Compassionate Souls

Compassionate Souls
Raising the Next Generation to
Change the World

By JoAnn Farb

Lantern Books
A Division of Booklight Inc.

2000
Lantern Books
One Union Square West, Suite 201
New York, NY 10003

This book is intended for educational purposes only. It should not
be considered as personal medical advice. The author and publish-
er encourage readers to conduct their own exhaustive research
before making any lifestyle changes and assume no responsibility
for any choices made.

Printed in the United States of America

Library of Congress Cataloging-in-Publication Data

Farb, JoAnn
    Compassionate Souls : raising the next generation to change
        the world / by JoAnn Farb.
        p. cm.
    Includes bibliographical references. (p.).
    ISBN 1-930051-03-4 (pbk. : alk. paper)
    1. Parenting—Moral and ethical aspects—United States.
    2. Child rearing—Moral and ethical aspects—United States.
    3. Child psychology—United States.
    4. Social Values—Study and teaching—United States. I. Title
HQ755.8 .F37 2000
649'7—dc21

                                                    00-039088

Contents

Acknowledgments

FIRST AND FOREMOST, I AM GRATEFUL TO MY HUSBAND, Joe, for his encouragement and support, and for picking up the slack when I got really into writing this book. Joe—you set a good example for me in so many ways! Thank you for the life we have together.

To Martin Rowe, who saw the potential, and was willing to give wings to my thoughts. Writing *Compassionate Souls* has been tremendously soul-satisfying. Thank you!

I appreciate the love and support of my parents, Bernie and Judy Fremerman, and my in-laws, Jack and Shirley Farb. I know that at times our lifestyle choices present challenges for all of you and I really appreciate how you have honored our wishes. You mean so much to me. It touches my heart to see the love between all of you and our children. Thank you for being there for us and for setting a great example for both Joe and me of long-term, stable marriages. Mom and Dad, I believe many of the blessings I enjoy today are the result of the choices you made and examples you've set in raising me. You have given me a great foundation upon which to build my own philosophy.

A special thanks to my sisters, Leslie Kanefsky and Kerry Fremerman—my lifelong mirrors. You continue to show me parts of myself I never knew were there. I thought of you two often while writing this book. Your views and comments over the years have helped me to clarify exactly what I believe.

To Sue Havala, my friend and mentor. Thank you for your endless encouragement and for having a vision of me as a person with something to offer the world—even at those times when I have had little more on my mind than nursing, finding a clean diaper, and getting some sleep.

Thanks to all my playgroup friends. You have enriched my life so much with your friendship, ideas, and support for the road less traveled. I don't believe I'd ever have written a book like this if it weren't for knowing all of you!

Thanks to John and Ruth Ann Winslow, and to Karen and Bill Hart. Your examples as parents have taught me so much, and enriched my life beyond words. Everything you've ever told me I've thought about a great deal. You are the families I studied most intensely and for the longest term. Thank you for including me in so much—your friendship has been priceless.

Thanks also to the following friends, teachers, mentors, thinkers, and pillars of the community who have questioned, challenged, educated, or encouraged me in the things I've done: Leon and Karen Rappaport, Sidney Willens, LeAnn Howard, James Urban Ph.D., Tina Kolm, Karen Dooley, David Rosenberg, Maggie Melvin, Ann Usher, Karen Jacks, Heather Eckard-Lee, Richard and Ellie Dawson, H. Dean Jernigan, Pat Bates, Linda Wherle, Suzy Latare, Susie Fichman, Donna Jacobson, John Kurman, Rebecca Pryor, Larry Faulkin, Cathan and Robin Prinzing, Victoria Moran, Carolyn Zak, Heidi and Johnathon Benham, Donald Fremerman, Danny and Dianna Meissinger, Douglas Brooks M.D., Bob and Jeanie Beauchamp, Howard Lyman, Gloria Squittaro, Debra Wasserman, Charles Stahler, Reed Mangels, Kelly Beard-Tittone, Joanne Stepaniak, John McDougall M.D., Brian Graff, George Mackie, Robert Cohen, and James Dray.

A special thanks to Michael Klaper M.D., who even before I had met him contributed so much to me via his writings on vegan pregnancy and nutrition for children.

To my children, Sarina and Samantha—my greatest teachers yet—who have fulfilled my lifelong desire: to be a mother.

Introduction

THIS IS A BOOK ABOUT CONSCIOUS PARENTING. IT IS, therefore, a book about choices. Unlike previous generations, we have more choices as parents than at any time in history. Yet, since all choices have consequences, this is both a blessing and a challenge. Parenting today is hard!

Parents today have an awesome responsibility. We're not just raising children; we're raising the adults of tomorrow. How do we prepare them to live and make choices in the world of tomorrow when we can't even predict what that world will be like? Regardless of how things change, we all still want the same things for our children—vibrant health, a sense of purpose, a comfortable lifestyle, loving relationships, and membership in a compassionate community.

In some ways, it seems, we should be better able than at any time in history to create good lives for our children and ourselves. For the most part, the majority of people living in the United States—even those near the poverty level—are materially more comfortable than the middle class of fifty years ago: The economy is booming; there are lots of jobs; there are libraries full of books and computers offering a wealth of free information and inspiration to those savvy enough to utilize it. Moreover, research is illuminating the lifestyle choices that are likely to keep us free of disease.

Yet there is a widespread feeling that something is wrong. A 1995 report prepared by the Harwood Group, and commissioned by the Merck Family Fund, found that Americans from all backgrounds shared fundamental concerns about the values they see driving our society. People felt that materialism, greed, and selfishness were crowding out more meaningful values that nurture the family and community. Respondents felt they didn't want to give up their financial security or material comforts—but they did want more balance with the non-material rewards of life.

Isn't this true of many of us? We believe that everyone should be able to choose how to live; yet sometimes we condemn others (and subconsciously ourselves?) for over-consumption. We seem to know intuitively that our collective lifestyles are not sustainable. The contradictions immobilize us. They keep us from examining our behavior too closely.

To complicate the issue, children are different today, and any teacher who's been in the classroom for more then twenty years can confirm this. Attention spans are shorter; children show a growing lack of respect for others; as the age of puberty decreases, children are becoming sexualized at increasingly younger ages. When popular books tell us that peers have far more influence than we do on our children, we shudder at the thought of peer pressure pushing our children to do unwholesome things. Raging hormones ignited by racy advertising force children to cope with adult desires long before they have the emotional maturity to make wise decisions.

As a culture we are so caught up in the maelstrom of the technological revolution, so sedated by television, and so convinced that the way to quell that aching dissonance inside us is to have more, be more, or do more that we continue on, knowing that something is not right, but feeling unsure as to quite what the problem is. According to an article on December 17, 1999, in *USA Today*, children aged twelve and under influence in one way or another the spending of $500 billion. Advertisers know this and specifically target youngsters. And that saturation is not merely on radio or television: Magazines aimed at children advertise adult products; promotional toys tie into cartoons, television, and movies; logos are on everything. Even schools, desperate to make up budget shortfalls, are selling advertisers access to our children. What's a parent to do?

With few exceptions, physical and emotional health are not accidents, but are the natural consequences of certain conditions. Unfortunately, our lifestyle is inconsistent with our biological and spiritual needs. The conditions that are omnipresent in America today, and rapidly spreading throughout the world, aren't likely to facilitate development of either a healthy body or healthy emotions. The evidence is everywhere around us: Childhood obesity is at an all-time high; asthma rates continue to skyrocket; learning disabilities, eating disorders, autism, and childhood cancers seem to be increasing.

That you even picked up this book means you're concerned. Whether you agree or disagree with my philosophy is not important. No matter how your children have come into your family, I guarantee *Compassionate Souls* will give you much to think about. Because there are many paths to raising children to have a good life and we must each find the path consistent with our own fundamental nature, I ask you to use what is relevant and disregard the rest. In some way, however, our job as parents must be to help our child develop the ability to see him- or herself as having choices in life, and having the tools to wisely navigate those choices. *Compassionate Souls* offers one bridge across the abyss.

Compassionate Souls will give you tools for helping your children grow into compassionate, caring adults, who can think for themselves and exercise their freedom responsibly. As you read, you may feel that some of what I suggest, although perhaps a good idea, would simply be too difficult for you to implement in your life at this time. If you decide that it would be too challenging for you to make choices so out of step with what most everyone else is doing, consider that in making that decision you are in essence modeling a very powerful example for your children. It is our actions, not our words or beliefs, that wield the most influence with our offspring.

When our children see us going along with the mainstream out of convenience rather then conviction, we are laying the foundation for them to do the same with their peers. If you are lucky enough for your child to have a group of children around who are caring, respectful, and inner-directed, then this may not be a problem. But the odds increasingly are that you may not be so lucky.

One of our most important jobs as parents is to teach our children to think for themselves. This can happen only when we start by instilling our values in them. Then they have a safe place from which to develop their own. Purveyors of junk foods, toxic chemicals, noxious drugs, and damaging technologies certainly have no qualms about trying to influence our children to adopt their values, and if we are not clear and convincing, our children will get a very lopsided picture of their choices.

I challenge you, therefore, to think deeply about your life and think about the dreams you have for your children. Take a good look at where Western civilization is heading. Ask yourself: Are we, as a whole, becoming more peaceful, loving, and respectful? Are we learning the lessons of our past? If the answer is yes, then you can put down this book and walk away. If there is even a slight hesitation, I urge you to read on.

Chapter One
On Becoming a Parent .

SOME PEOPLE, LOOKING BACK AT THE 1960s, ATTRIBUTE the revolutionary spirit of young people at that time to the ideas popularized by Dr. Benjamin Spock. Dr. Spock, a pediatrician and author of the world-renowned *Dr. Spock's Baby and Child Care*, advocated a much more compassionate style of parenting than was previously the norm.

Children who came of age in the Sixties were the first generation whose parents were widely influenced by Dr. Spock's ideas. While there were negative aspects to some of what the Sixties brought, there were some important and strikingly positive things that happened then as well. The Sixties were a time of incredible optimism; the younger generation truly believed they had the power to make a difference. This was the time of the civil rights and women's movements, peace protests, and other activism for social change. It was the youth of the Sixties who later founded The Farm in Summertown, Tennessee—a unique intentional community that keeps a wholly vegetarian (vegan) diet. The Farm went on to become the birthplace of the Book Publishing Company, which specializes in vegan and vegetarian cookbooks. The Farm is also known for its promotion of home birth and midwifery, and for teaching poor owners of forested land how to make money growing shiitake mushrooms without destroying the trees. These are good things, and give me great hope for the future. The Farm, although over thirty years old, is still quietly and profoundly changing our culture.

I mention The Farm and Dr. Spock because together they represent the kinds of parenting and social activism I will be talking about in *Compassionate Souls*. While a more compassionate approach to parenting was only one of the factors that sparked the great social changes characteristic of the Sixties, I believe it was a critical one. A widespread awareness of the impact of our civilization on the environment was another.

While the Sixties are long gone, the generation who came of age in that decade are now our leaders. These "baby boomers" continue to be a major force in America. Although we have backslid on some of what the Sixties stood for, the beliefs of those years are now embedded in the cultural psyche of all Americans. When the pendulum swings back again, the progress made in the Sixties will serve as the foundation for even greater strides.

A New Parenting Revolution: Attachment-Style

We are now on the cusp of a new parenting revolution, and this one is being sparked by the ideas of another pediatrician—Dr. William Sears. Together with his wife, Martha, Dr. Sears has written over a dozen books addressing different aspects of the philosophy known as "attachment-style parenting." Attachment-style parenting is based upon parents forming and nurturing a very strong attachment to their newborns. If the first meeting of parents with their new child is not interfered with, the Searses argue, the degree of bonding that takes place will spontaneously encourage the normal and passionate attachment of parents to their child. This strong attachment will facilitate the behaviors our biology craves. Sleeping with your infant (known as family bed), keeping your infant in mostly continuous contact with a loving adult's body—as most humans in non-Western cultures automatically do—(known as "baby wearing"), breastfeeding on request and extended breastfeeding, and prompt compassionate responses to an infant's needs form the foundation of attach-ment-parenting. A mother, suggest the Searses, who has securely bonded with her newborn is not likely to leave her in the care of others. This encourages successful nursing and builds security in her baby. A secure infant whose biologically programmed needs are fully met is free to turn her entire attention to mastering herself and learning about the world around her.

However, if the baby is removed from the mother's arms for hos- . pital routines or treatment—especially during the first few hours after birth—a critical window of opportunity to easily form a strong attachment is missed. This is why understanding our birth options and their consequences is so important. Humans are designed to grow and mature in response to certain cues. A natural birth starts us on the path to realizing our fullest potential by increasing or decreasing the odds that our fundamental needs are met.

The Searses' strong Christian faith is part of their parenting, although this may not be obvious to the reader unless you happen to see their book as specifically on Christian parenting. However, while the Searses attempt to model their parenting upon Jesus' compassion, most of today's parenting books aimed at people of faith seem on the other hand to emphasize parental control, punishment, and the rigorous scheduling of babies' lives. This type of less-responsive parenting is relatively new to our species and, I believe, is inconsistent with our biological programming. The vast majority of cultures throughout history have spontaneously cared for infants in a way that nurtures a strong attachment and builds trust by meeting a baby's needs. Other primates do this as well.

What should be emphasized here is that while the Searses' discipline is extremely compassionate, it is not lax. As parents they set firm limits. The Searses simply believe, however, that we should treat our children in a way that's respectful of us and respectful of them and that serves as a model of how humans should interact with one another. I talk more about birthing and parenting infants later on, and more about the Searses' parenting methods in Chapter Six.

Learning about Parenting

When I was growing up, I had an aunt whom I respected tremendously. She was beautiful and witty, but also terribly intimidating. She had this way about her that just made everyone want to stay on her good side. Although I was a challenging child for any adult, around this aunt I was always on my best behavior. My aunt's two little girls, my cousins, were the most delightful and obedient children I'd ever met and were the talk of the family. Everyone loved being around them because they were so well-behaved. In contrast to how my cousins were raised, discipline at my house was less consistent and this showed in my behavior. I was quite aware that while most adults adored my cousins, I was not the apple of everyone's eye. As I saw how adults responded to my cousins, I came to the conclusion that, when I was a mother, I would want my children to be well-disciplined and to feel liked. So I studied how my aunt disciplined her children. She never yelled, but she had a look. When she gave an order you knew she meant business. Several times, I remember seeing my cousins failing to respond quickly enough to their mother's instructions, and as a result becoming the immediate recipients of a swat on the behind. "This," I thought to my naive self, "is how to raise delightful children." I will talk more about discipline and coping with difficult children later on.

I used to think, when trying to understand how we form our beliefs, that certain influences or exposure to ideas at critical times were the reason we adopt our own particular perspectives on things. While writing this book, I wondered why, for instance, I have always had such a strong desire to breastfeed my babies—long before I had adequate facts to compel me to do so. I attribute this desire to something that happened when I was nine years old. One of the other children in my class had an eight-month-old baby sister who occasionally visited our classroom while her mother helped out. Something about the way that mother connected with her baby touched me very deeply. I saw this mother nursing and we also had a few discussions about natural childbirth. Despite having almost no exposure to any other nursing couples until I was much older, this experience laid the foundation for me to become a passionate breastfeeding advocate. I think often about this mother now and feel deep appreciation for her example. Yet I don't think she influenced me *per se*. I feel that what I saw in her resonated with who I fundamentally am.

Thus, what I used to interpret as an external influence, I now see as merely fertilizing a dormant seed within. The fact that I was capable of being affected by this mother and baby I now explain as reflecting a combination of who I was from the moment I came into this world and the cumulative early experiences that shaped my perceptions of myself and others. I am ever conscious of the example I may be setting for children I meet everywhere I go. Regardless of what their upbringing is like, I know I could be for them what this mother was for me.

As I have studied what I consider "successful" families—that is, families who seem to have well-behaved, usually happy, considerate children, and an abundance of love among all members—they all seem to have one thing in common. They see themselves as part of a larger community that has clearly defined principles and ethics that guide their behavior. Many of these families derive this guidance from participation with an organized religious group; but I have also seen non-religious families which are dedicated to specific issues or committed to giving something back to the community embody these same characteristics.

Before marriage, my husband and I had frequent discussions about what we wanted for our children. We talked about the strengths and weaknesses of our own upbringings. We both felt very blessed by all the positive things our own families of origin had instilled in us—a feeling of being wanted and loved, of being able to make choices in life and assume full responsibility for the consequences of those choices, a strong work ethic, a belief in the importance of giving back to the community, and a love of learning. There were also specific ways as parents we felt we could and would do better—like most of us, we have more information and vastly greater choices as parents than our parents had.

Although the seeds were planted long before I met my husband, I could never have blossomed into the mother I am today without his support and encouragement. Some of the choices we have made for our family are simply too different from what society generally endorses and from what our extended families embrace. Although we feel there are compelling reasons why these choices were good for our children and us, it really took both of us wanting to do these things for me to have the commitment to stay the course on such a path.

I am grateful I had sufficient information and knew myself well enough prior to meeting my husband to know I wanted to raise my children on a really healthy diet and to know what that meant we would and would not eat. I am also grateful I had thought at length about the values I consider central in my life and those I wanted to share with my children. It would have been devastating to me personally not to be able to shape my home and family life in a way consistent with my life principles.

That these things resonated with my husband also enabled us to get married. I strongly urge anyone contemplating family life to examine these issues before making a commitment with a partner and choosing to raise children.

Chapter Two
Conscious Birth

WHEN I BECAME PREGNANT WITH MY FIRST CHILD, I had been following a vegan diet for about two years. (A vegan diet involves the consumption of no animal products at all.) I was feeling healthy and assumed this would be the best diet for my developing baby. When my prenatal visits with the ob/gyn started, I explained my diet to him. He not only wasn't concerned, but didn't even seem to care what I, or any pregnant woman, ate. (I later learned that this particular doctor had been nicknamed "Dr. C-section" by other women. A poor diet may increase the need for interventions during childbirth, which can culminate in being given a caesarean section.)

From the moment my husband and I planned to get pregnant, I began reading everything I could about pregnancy. I started with the public library, which had a pretty good selection for initial reading but didn't last me long enough. Desperate for more material, I read as widely as possible—even the books on caesarean sections and twin pregnancies, even though I was sure I was having neither.

La Leche League
During my second trimester I heard about La Leche League. Originally, I had mistakenly believed that La Leche was only an organization to turn to if I found myself having difficulty with breastfeeding. Fortunately a friend told me that La Leche League is

actually a source of information and support for a full range of mothering-related issues. I started attending meetings. La Leche League (LLL) was founded in 1956 by a group of seven nursing mothers concerned that breastfeeding rates in the United States had dropped to around twenty percent of new mothers. By 1964, LLL had published its well-known book *Womanly Art of Breastfeeding*, had organized in several other countries, and had sponsored an international conference in Chicago attended by over 500 people. Today LLL boasts over 3,000 local groups in the United States, operates a twenty-four-hour help line, and offers extensive literature covering a wide range of topics related to better mothering through breastfeeding. There is information about contacting them in the Resources section at the back of this book.

LLL meetings take place in public places or homes and provide priceless support. They follow a set format that includes presentation of information on four specific topics (one per meeting) and these rotate, so you need only to attend four consecutive times to cover the basic material. The meetings are free and open to anyone—even if you're not a member—and nursing infants are always welcome.

An important component of each meeting is the informal sharing among mothers. After the meeting time officially ends, informal discussion among the mothers usually continues. It was in this setting and during this time that I heard the real scoop on various doctors, hospitals, schools, birth clinics, childbirth education classes, and more. Another benefit I experienced was access to LLL's extraordinarily wide-ranging library of books. I found much more useful information in the books that LLL stocked than what was usually on the shelf at my public library. By the time I had exhausted LLL's inventory, my husband and I were starting our weekly Bradley childbirth education class, which I had heard about from a mother I met at a league meeting.

When we first looked into attending a childbirth education class, my husband and I were quickly able to narrow down our choices.

We ruled out all classes taught in affiliation with obstetrical practices and hospitals, since at that time we were going on our intuition that these would likely be under pressure to teach only the things that would make us "good patients"—in other words, compliant and unquestioning of "normal" procedures. As it turned out, I have since heard from instructors who teach these classes that patients are frequently grouped in classes according to who their doctor is, so that the doctors can give specific instructions to the teacher about topics they do not want covered with their patients. Teachers who fail to honor the doctor's wishes risk having the doctor no longer refer patients to them. It is, therefore, important to find out exactly what the classes are about, before going or not going to them!

Bradley
Bradley childbirth education is a comprehensive program using nationally certified instructors independent of hospitals to teach couples about natural childbirth and give them the tools to make informed decisions during pregnancy and birth. The Bradley philosophy encourages active participation in labor, avoidance of drugs, immediate and continuous contact with your new baby, preparation for emergencies, and informed consumer choices. Our Bradley instructor also had a lending library of books containing difficult-to-find information on circumcision, vaccination, ultrasound, homebirth, and water births. Having read so much, we were in a good position to make decisions about the choices that lay ahead.

The Importance of Education
I cannot emphasize enough the importance of educating yourself early on. If you wait until you are halfway through your pregnancy to start learning about the options you have for where to give birth and what technology you do or don't want used on you and the baby, you will be at a serious disadvantage. Your medical practitioner will feel compelled (due to an education that disproportionately

represents the interests of drug and medical device manufacturers as well as a fear of malpractice) to use a vast array of usually unnecessary technologies that could make you very vulnerable to additional risky medical interventions. Being informed of the risks and benefits of all these procedures puts you in a better position to make your own choices.

A minor intervention may increase the chance of a second intervention being used. This, in turn, can create a snowball effect, which ultimately may put a woman and her baby at risk of something serious. For instance, hospitals generally won't allow laboring women to eat. The reasoning is that if the mother requires general anesthesia she could throw up and then possibly aspirate vomit into her lungs, which may lead to pneumonia. On the other hand, not allowing a laboring woman to eat increases the chance that her baby will be born with low blood sugar. Low blood sugar in the newborn justifies giving him formula immediately. This, in turn, reduces the amount of colostrum the baby gets, which normally acts as a laxative removing bilirubin from his system. This, in turn, can lead to jaundice, which justifies the baby being taken away from the parents and isolated in the neonatal intensive care unit with the baby's eyes covered while he or she is exposed for a day or two to bilirubin lights. Aside from this being traumatic for the baby, it can interfere with bonding and decrease the chance for successful breastfeeding. Having a vague idea that something might not really be best for your baby will not give you the strength of conviction to stand up to a room full of doctors and nurses intent on getting you to comply with hospital procedure.

Soon after I started seeing my ob/gyn (the infamous Dr. C-section), I was told it was time for my gestational diabetes test. Thanks to my Bradley childbirth class I had learned enough to know the dangers of this test and I declined to take it. The test itself requires the pregnant woman to fast overnight and then drink a concentrated glucose solution. Blood samples are drawn at regular intervals over the course of the next several hours. Then the woman is finally allowed to eat again.

Unfortunately, because the results can be highly influenced by the woman's diet of just the few previous days, the test is fraught with error. It also seems highly dubious to deprive a healthy pregnant woman of food, especially when, if she is careful to eat a low-fat, whole-foods diet, and eschews refined sugars, she will already be at low risk for diabetes. Plus, that dose of glucose could be a huge shock to both her and her developing baby. Several women who took this test have told me that after drinking the glucose they could feel their baby in their uterus become incredibly active to an alarming point.

Because of these concerns, I refused to submit to the routine glucose tolerance test. This, of course, provoked great concern from the doctor and his staff. I, therefore, asked them what they would do if the tests showed I had gestational diabetes. The doctor and his staff handed me a diet sheet and told me I would be encouraged to follow it. If the test showed I had an extreme case, they said, I might even have to take insulin shots for the duration of my pregnancy. (What they didn't say, but I know to be true, is that my chart would get the label "high risk" and I would be subjected to additional interventions and restrictions during labor.)

I looked at the diet they had put together. Meat, dairy, and refined processed foods were part of the menu for every day. In addition, diet pop was allowed daily as well. I mentally compared this to the way I was now eating: cooked whole grains, lots of salads with low-fat vinegar-and-tofu–based dressings; lots of fresh vegetables and fruits; occasional nuts and seeds; some olive oil in food preparation, and moderate amounts of tofu, tempeh, soymilk, and beans. Occasionally I would indulge in some vegan alternative to popular junky desserts. My diet had no artificial sweeteners, colors, flavorings, or preservatives, and had very little hydrogenated or saturated fat.

I tried to point out to the doctor and his staff that the diet I was now following was much better than the diet they would recommend for gestational diabetes. I tried to explain to them how simply eating a lot of fat and not much fiber or complex carbohydrates for a few days would increase insulin resistance in most people and yield a positive result on their test. Unfortunately, my arguments fell on deaf ears and, amid the threats of "You could hurt your baby," I was forced to stand my ground.

Ensuring a Safe Birth

During this time, my husband and I started to get a firmer sense of what we did and did not want for the birth of our baby. First and foremost, of course, we wanted the birth to be safe. As we learned more about the risks of routine procedures, I would convey to Dr. C-section our wishes to avoid these. He would nod, pat me on the head, and say: "Don't you worry, I'll take care of everything." But I did worry! I got the distinct feeling that he wasn't even hearing anything I was saying. Finally one day, I boldly asked him what percentage of his clients ended up getting C-sections. He smiled patronizingly and told me that I didn't need to worry my little head about that. So I repeated my question. This time he replied that whatever happened to other women had absolutely no bearing on what would happen to me. Despite my persistence, he flat-out refused to answer my question. I left the exam room and went straight to the nurses' station. "Maybe his staff will tell me," I thought. I was wrong.

In one final attempt I called the hospital Dr. C-section was affiliated with, only to strike out for the third time. They were willing to give me the hospital's overall C-section rate (twenty-five percent of all births at that hospital were delivered by caesarian section) but said they were not authorized to release statistics on any particular doctor.

By now, we were starting to rethink our entire plans for the birth. We knew hospitals were the most likely place that one might pick up a deadly infection. Our own home, unkempt as it might be, was at least filled with only our own germs. My immune system had already worked out how to deal with these, and since my antibodies would be flowing to our baby via the placenta and my milk, this offered a high-degree of protection for birth and afterwards. As I said earlier, most procedures that had become standard in the hospital carried specific risks. While some technologies could be life-saving when used appropriately, it had, because of the number of malpractice cases, become the norm for doctors to employ many of these procedures with every pregnancy and birth—even those that were low risk. By doing this, if there was a bad outcome to the pregnancy and delivery, the doctor could always say that he or she had done exactly what was usual and customary, and would likely not be found liable. If the patient was injured by some technology she really hadn't needed, the doctor could still say he or she was following standard practice and again would likely be vindicated. We were very aware that there were no guarantees that our strategy was the correct one, but given our focus on healthy lifestyle choices, we felt much better betting on nature than on technology.

The list of interventions that we did not want was growing. We wanted no IV during labor since I wanted to be able to move freely in order to work with my body. I was also concerned that use of an IV during labor might increase my risk of contracting an infection. Even more of a concern was the fact that it provided an open portal for administration of drugs I might get before I had a chance to refuse them. We also wanted no Doppler stethoscopes used, since these essentially employed the same technology as sonograms, and sonograms had been shown by some studies to elicit unusual changes in cells. Since a female baby in utero already has all the egg cells her body will ever make in her ovaries, negative effects of sonograms might not be seen for another generation. We didn't want any fetal monitors used because these too utilized ultrasound. We had read data that show that when fetal monitors are used across the board on

low-risk women there is no improvement in outcomes but there are
false alarms leading to increased interventions and C-sections.

Unless it was a matter of life and death, we wanted our baby to
be placed immediately on my body after delivery and allowed to
nurse. Doing this would speed up expulsion of the placenta, reduce
my risk of hemorrhage, and get valuable colostrum into our baby
right away. We wanted our baby not to be taken from our arms or
get eye drops that might blur her vision and interfere with bonding.
(My husband and I are both healthy and monogamous, so we
weren't worried about STDs.) We did not want the umbilical cord
cut until it finished pulsating, since the extra volume of blood that
it delivered would contain as much iron as a formula-fed baby can
obtain from iron-fortified formula in six months.

Our concerns for the birth extended beyond just the health
issues—we wanted our whole family to be comfortable with our
choices. The birth of our child would be a major rite of passage for
us, a life-affirming and life-changing event, and we didn't want to
pass the decision-making on to someone else. As a mother-to-be and
as a woman, I didn't want to be treated as merely a pelvis. As I discovered the closer I got to delivery, the dehumanizing rituals prevalent in modern medicine were becoming rather obvious. We didn't
want our baby's birth to accommodate the whims and routines of an
institution.

Our Midwife
The more we thought about it, we felt that birth was a sacred event
that should take place in our spiritual center—our home. A hospital
just didn't seem like a very appropriate place to welcome this beautiful new being that would be a part of our lives forever. Eventually
we got enough of the medicalized approach to childbirth and trad-
ed in Dr. C-section for a fantastic lay-midwife and made a decision
to have our baby at home. Our midwife recommended that we also
make an appointment with a particular doctor in our area who pro-

vides hospital back-up for her clients—just in case they decide to transfer into the hospital. Having a doctor sympathetic to home birth should you need a hospital could make a huge difference in the type of treatment you would get, she said. This doctor, a specialist in family practice, has turned out to be wonderful for our whole family. He respects our right to use him as a consultant and make our own health care decisions.

Our prenatal visits with the midwife usually lasted over an hour. She was gentle, nurturing, and never rushed. She would feel my swollen abdomen with her hands, and tell us the position the baby was in. I really looked forward to our weekly visits! After she located the heartbeat with her old-fashioned stethoscope, both my husband and I were encouraged to listen. She allotted plenty of time for us to ask her absolutely anything and everything we could think of.

For the most part my pregnancy was uneventful and healthy. Labor, however, was not what I had expected. It went on for three days due to unforeseen interference from a prior tailbone injury. After dilating to eight centimeters, I figured I was finally close to having the baby. (Ten centimeters, about the size of a baby's head, is considered fully dilated.) But then something I had never heard of happened—my cervix closed back up. The contractions continued for two nights, and, with no baby appearing, I was totally demoralized. The contractions were hard and coming every couple of minutes. I felt them entirely in my lower back. It had been impossible to sleep through the contractions, but I was so tired that I was passing out for two to three minutes in between them.

When morning came, we abandoned plans for a homebirth and went to the hospital so I could get some pain relief. My midwife suggested that I refuse all other pain medication and only get an epidural, since it offered the most reliable pain relief and would have the least impact on the baby. I was thankful we had arranged for a back-up doctor, since he made our hospital visit so much better. Despite the pain and fatigue, I walked into the hospital and mentally saw myself putting on my boxing gloves. I must have been quite a sight! In addition to being in a defensive posture, I was also telling every single person that I saw in white (some of whom were probably janitors) that I wanted an epidural and wanted one now. Once I had made the mental leap to accept a drugged birth, I wanted pain relief *now*. However, I was still scared they would attempt to force unnecessary procedures on us. To my surprise, however, the nurse said to me: "Oh you're a homebirth family? Well then, we'll just bring you the paperwork to sign off on any procedures you don't want." It was such a relief! (My midwife has since told me that this respectful treatment was due to who our doctor was rather than the particular hospital we went to.)

As soon as we got into our room, the medical staff examined me and discovered that I was fully dilated. So instead of pain relief they helped me into a pushing position. I regained my motivation to eschew the drugs. Two hours later, when I had still made no progress and the contractions had nearly stopped, they checked me again, and found my cervix had closed back to about four centimeters. At this point the doctor suggested that he puncture my bag of waters. I agreed. As hoped, this got the contractions going again. But by this time, I had had enough! Going through transition twice (the most intense part of labor) had pretty much sunk my commitment to a drug-free birth. This time I was screaming for an epidural.

When the anesthesiologist came in, he explained to me that there was a small risk of permanent paralysis from the epidural and a higher risk of lingering back pain or long-term headaches. I knew all this. I was sitting up as he started to place the needle into my spine. He emphasized the importance of my remaining perfectly still while he inserted the needle. I did this, until an intense contraction came on. Struggling to manage the pain, I moved slightly. The doctor stopped what he was doing and yelled at me: "If you move again the whole deal is off! You won't get an epidural!" Fortunately, he was able to insert the needle before the next contraction. I prayed that neither my baby nor myself would be harmed.

Fairly shortly afterward, the entire lower half of my body went numb. This completely stopped the contractions, which, at that point, was a good thing. After two nights of almost no sleep I immediately passed out. When I woke up about four hours later I felt much better, but found that I was still no closer to having a baby. Since my water had already broken, breaking the baby's bag of water was no longer an option to get things going. My doctor suggested pitocin, a hormone that can bring on labor but also carries risks. I agreed to it. It didn't do much, so the dose was doubled and then the contractions came on fast. However, were it not for the monitor, I wouldn't have known, since I had absolutely no sensation from my waist down, so strong was the epidural. It was an eerie thing to be giving birth and be so detached from it. I felt disconnected and removed from my baby.

At that point I encountered one of the risks of pitocin—the monitors started to indicate that the baby was being stressed. I could tell that the mood in the room was turning serious. The anesthesiologist made a joke to my husband about how I was going to be getting a smiley face on my belly. (He was obviously unaware that no one else considered a C-section something funny.) We were literally minutes away from surgery when I started to feel something in my bottom. Thinking the epidural might be wearing off, I notified the nurses that I was feeling something. There was one thing I knew for sure: We had come this far (in terms of the interventions and drugs) and there was no way I wanted to feel any more of the back pain that had characterized this labor.

I heard someone yell, "Check her!" and then I heard, "There's a head!" By this time all I could think about was that my cervix had closed up twice before. This was the third time I'd dilated; I needed to push my baby out now, before my cervix closed up again. The problem, however, was that because I was totally numb I couldn't even feel myself push. I kept trying different things and asking the doctor whether what I was doing was pushing. I completely relied on the people around me for feedback as to whether my body was doing what I was trying to get it to do. Since I had no idea when my contractions were occurring, I had no idea when to push. I simply pushed as hard and continuously as I possibly could.

It worked. Sarina came out, perfectly fine at seven pounds eleven ounces, and started nursing immediately. I was filled with love. Instantly, nothing else mattered as long as she was in my arms. I did, however, have a huge tear in my perineum that required stitches. (I later learned that one of the keys to not tearing is to allow the baby to come out slowly and only push with the contractions, so that the perineum can slowly stretch to accommodate the baby.) Knowing that our baby was much more likely to contract an infection in the hospital, we were anxious to return home. The doctor told me that as soon as the epidural wore off, we could leave, and about three hours later we were back home.

What We Learned about Birthing

Our entire birthing experience had an interesting effect on our attitude. When we'd first decided to transfer into the hospital we had felt defeated and sad about giving up our dream of a homebirth. After it was all over, we felt victorious that we'd narrowly avoided a C-section. I experienced not a moment of postpartum depression, which I have heard may be one outcome of a woman being violated by the experience of birthing in the hospital and feeling powerless. Except for my brief and unpleasant interactions with the anesthesiologist, I have to say that my hospital birth experience was far better than I'd ever imagined it could be. I felt I'd been given a choice about everything that was done to me. I'd been fully informed and had done my best to avoid drugs and other interventions. I was also glad that the hospital and the epidural were there when I chose them. I fully believe that given the type of labor I had, if we had started out at the hospital I would definitely have been given a C-section—hospitals won't let you labor for as long as I did to get my first baby out vaginally!

My Second Pregnancy

Since that time I've been through a second pregnancy. This one was very different, perhaps because I had an energetic preschooler to care for or perhaps because I was four years older. I had also just come through the most stressful year of my life, which had culminated in moving from a home we loved. Whatever the cause, I felt lousy right from the beginning. My level of fitness was lower and my diet probably not as good as it had been with my first pregnancy— something I didn't even realize until about my last trimester. After I made some changes, things improved. (I will discuss this further in Chapter Five.)

As my due date neared, I was feeling better—as if I actually might have enough energy to get through a long labor. Again we were planning a homebirth, but this time I had lined up additional help. My chiropractor agreed to be on call and actually come to my house if needed, and give me an adjustment if labor got stuck. My acupuncturist told me I could call him when labor started and he would come give me a treatment to facilitate birth.

About noon a few days after my due date, I was running errands with my then four-year-old daughter when labor started. We made one last stop at the grocery store to stock up on a few things before heading home. (It would be a long time before I was in a grocery store again. I had to have one last spree.) The contractions, though bearable, were strong enough that I had to lean on the grocery cart for support. We hurried home. I was a little nervous about what I would do if labor picked up while driving home, since we lived in a rural area about ten minutes' drive away, and part of the route was gravel. Fortunately, I had no strong contractions while driving.

My husband was home when we arrived and a few hours later our midwife joined us. She thought I was in very early labor and settled into the guest room for a nap. By six o'clock in the evening, the contractions had intensified and I needed my midwife's support. She showed me how to breathe with the contractions and conserve my energy. When I grew weary of one position, she assisted me in finding something new. Remembering my marathon labor with my first child, I didn't think I'd be able to keep it up all night again—even though my midwife kept indicating that we still had a long way to go.

It seemed to me as if these contractions were coming right on the heels of my last labor. I reflected on how fast four years had gone. Around eight o'clock my acupuncturist arrived. By this time, contractions were coming every couple of minutes. I felt fine in between them, but when one came I was adamant that no one in the room should talk or even move. It took all my concentration to stay on top of the contraction and not let it overwhelm me with pain. As long as nothing distracted me, I could do it. So, in between the contractions, my acupuncturist read my pulses and treated a few points. He was very conservative in what he did, and then told me that was all he was going to do for the moment.

My midwife suggested I try laboring in the Jacuzzi for a change of scenery; and she was right to suggest it. The warm water instantly made me feel better. My midwife did her first internal exam. (Since internal exams are possible sources of infection, she never did these during prenatal visits, and in labor doesn't do them until things have progressed sufficiently.) I was only partially dilated. However, on my next contraction she gently stretched my cervix and it opened to almost ten centimeters. However, after the contraction ended we lost all the ground we had gained. On the next contraction she continued to apply pressure to the cervix after the contraction ended. I remained dilated. After just a few more of these, my baby's head popped out underwater. Because I had been totally numb for the birth of my first baby, this was the first time I actually experienced what it was like to have a baby come through me—and it was an amazing experience, beyond the realm of language.

I had the sensation of a box shape moving through my body, and then a feeling of opening up that evoked memories of sensations I had experienced twenty years previously in a few psychedelic moments. I believe that part of what I felt was my baby's soul actually separating from mine. It was magic.

Birth: A Family Affair
Just as the baby's head crowned (where you can see the head but it hasn't fully emerged) one of my friends, who had been there for the purpose of caring for our four-year-old, went and got our sleeping child and brought her to us. Sarina was instantly wide-awake and thrilled to be witnessing the birth. (For months she had been asking to be present.) At 9:30 p.m., our second baby was born underwater in our Jacuzzi tub. When the baby was fully out, I heard my husband's voice, full of love and emotion, tell me it was a girl. At that point, our four-year-old spoke up and her words and intonation will be forever etched in my memory of that occasion: "Oh," she said. "That's just what I was hoping for!"

The midwife brought her to the surface and helped me to turn over (I had given birth on my hands and knees). This actually proved to be very challenging. The umbilical cord was unusually short and it had just barely enough play to allow Sammi to be placed at my breast while we waited for the placenta to be expelled. It seemed forever for the placenta to come out! But about forty-five minutes later it finally did and only then was the cord cut. (This reduces the risk of hemorrhage in the mother.) We all dried off and moved to the bed, where we felt infinitely more comfortable. Sammi weighed eight pounds fourteen ounces. Her Apgars (an index named for anesthesiologist Virginia Apgar to measure color, heart rate, stimulus response, muscle tone, and respiration in newborns) were perfect. She was a chubby little thing. Although her eyes were wide open, Sammi seemed somewhat in shock. Looking back, I have the feeling that the acupuncture treatment sped things up perhaps a little too much for Sammi. (Although I was extremely pleased that the labor had gone so quickly, I too had a vague feeling that it had happened so fast as to seem surreal.)

Our midwife brought the placenta over to the bed for us to see. She showed us all the different parts—the side that had been against Sammi and the part that had been against my womb. Everything looked normal except that it was very small. For a baby that was almost nine pounds, the placenta was about half the size my midwife expected. Nevertheless, it got the job done.

Hospital versus Home; Medicated versus Natural

My husband and I are not planning on having any more children. I look back on my birth experiences with a mixture of relief and sadness that I won't have to go through any of it again. Initially I had chosen natural childbirth (at home) because I didn't want my babies to come into this world under the influence of drugs and was concerned about the myriad risks associated with hospital births. To some degree I saw myself sacrificing my own comfort for the best interests of my baby. But after having gone through both a drug-intensive hospital birth and a natural homebirth, I can honestly say that, if I were to give birth again, I would choose a natural birth not only for my baby but more so for myself. There is something extraordinary about giving birth consciously—even if in pain—and I will always treasure it.

As my experience in both hospital and home attests, however, it is very important to know what interventions are available, and to be clear what you want and when. A good hospital and doctor should always make you aware of your choices, and should respect your wishes. It is essential to remain conscious of your choices and your experience—so you can fully welcome your child into the world.

Chapter Three
Breastfeeding

PRIOR TO ABOUT 1880 MOST BABIES WERE NURSED BY either their mothers or wet-nurses. It was not until advances in sanitation, development of uncontaminated feeders, and significant alterations were made to cow's milk that artificial feeding became a possibility. Although most people assume that the ingredients used to make infant formula are selected based upon ingredients that provide superior nutrition, this is not the case.

You might find it alarming, but many of the ingredients in formulas are there because they're cheap and widely available. For instance, the fats most often used in formula are cottonseed oil, beef tallow, and coconut oil. When artificial feeding first took off, formulas were most often based upon cow's milk, because a booming dairy industry had surplus milk and was looking for additional markets. When alternatives to cow's milk were needed for babies with allergies to dairy products, a growing soybean industry positioned itself to take advantage of this new market.

Formula for Disaster
Although the initial impetus in developing artificial milks had been to save the lives of foundlings, by the 1900s formula companies were looking to the global market for profits. The companies worked to make bottle-feeding the norm and skillful marketing made mothers around the world (and particularly in developing

countries) believe that bottle-feeding was superior and more modern than breastfeeding. The medical profession collaborated in this, lured by the desire to standardize and control infant feeding and gave bottle-feeding an air of legitimacy.

Television provided a powerful new medium to accompany the billboard and radio advertising that already bombarded the masses with pro–bottle-feeding messages. Doctors were offered research grants and gifts in exchange for distributing free formula samples to their patients. Formula companies hired professional nurses to visit new mothers. Wearing their nurses' uniform, and being paid commissions that exceeded the usual pay of nurses, these women were often mistaken for hospital personnel. They had liberal access to new mothers to promote artificial milk as superior to breast milk.

As formula sales grew and women abandoned breastfeeding, malnutrition and infant mortality increased. Underdeveloped countries lacking sanitary water for mixing with the formula were hit especially hard. Women who couldn't read the instructions on formula bottles failed to mix the powdered formula properly or to boil the water first. This situation continues today. Poor families may spend up to half of their income on formula, trying to stretch the formula further by over-diluting it with water. All of these factors increase the incidence of what has become known as "bottle-baby disease"—a combination of diarrhea, dehydration, and malnutrition resulting from unsafe bottle-feeding. According to the United Nations Children's Fund (UNICEF), one and a half million babies die each year because they are not breastfed.

Most fathers and mothers in our culture are dangerously unconscious of the forces influencing them in the choices they make for their children. Nowhere is this more evident than when it comes to feeding their babies. As I began to appreciate the benefits of breastfeeding through education and then practice, I also started to learn about the multitudes of insidious ways that formula companies have attempted to create larger and larger markets for their products. For example, some manufacturers of infant formula have donated money and free architectural services to hospitals building new maternity wings, and then have had their architects design the new wing with the mothers' rooms and the nursery as far apart as possible—thus making it inconvenient for nurses to bring the babies to their mothers to nurse.

In the United States we are rightly proud of our freedom—especially when it comes to a woman choosing how she will feed her baby. Yet most women have too little information regarding the benefits of breastfeeding and the risks of artificial feeding to make a sound judgment. By not understanding all the subtle ways bottle-feeding is encouraged today, women are hardly free to make a knowledgeable choice at all.

We in the United States are fortunate to have access to medicines and technologies that can save the lives of most babies who routinely develop diarrhea or become severely ill from common infections while being fed formula. Even so, according to a 1989 study conducted by the U.S. National Institute of Environmental Health Sciences, roughly four of every thousand infants born in the United States die each year because they are not breastfed. Diarrhea and other common infections are usually minor in a fully breastfed infant. Women in developing countries, however, who succumb to slick advertising and abandon breastfeeding thinking they're doing what is best for their baby have no safety net if their child falls ill from bottle-feeding. Since formula-feeding costs well over $1,000 per year (not including the extra expense at the doctor's office to treat the more-likely-to-get-sick baby) this is a considerable expense in both health and money.

During my first pregnancy, I was inundated with propaganda from formula companies advocating their products. For my second pregnancy, I was careful to keep my name clear of every mailing list. I made one mistake when purchasing an outfit at a maternity store and gave them my due date (so they could notify me of sales), after they promised me they wouldn't sell or rent my name. Exactly two weeks later, a barrage of advertising began appearing in my mailbox—the overwhelming majority of which was formula advertising, full of free samples. Mysteriously, the samples were always for a formula product targeted exactly to my baby's age.

Every time one of these things arrived it would infuriate me. How many mothers and babies had had their breastfeeding sabotaged by this? I asked myself. If a women is not well-informed, she won't know all the different things that can damage her ability to produce milk. For instance, until breastfeeding is well-established, a woman needs to have her baby sucking every two hours for at least ten minutes on each breast. (Proper positioning of the baby is crucial to success, too.) What happens if, however, a woman comes home from the hospital and is nursing but doesn't have much support? Her baby is crying, she may be tense and her nipples sore. Her husband tries to be helpful. "Here," he says, showing her the free formula samples. "Why don't you get some rest and I'll feed our baby."

What this well-meaning couple doesn't realize is that, without the baby sucking, the woman's milk supply won't be adequately stimulated. The next time she tries to nurse, there may be less milk. Then the baby gets frustrated—nursing takes work, compared to having a bottle just drip into their mouth! So the parents try one more bottle. This is the beginning of the end. Without someone knowledgeable to help the mother and father, they will believe that the mother doesn't have enough milk.

According to the book *Milk, Money, and Madness* by Naomi Baumslag M.D., formula sales have tripled over the past ten years and the industry is now bigger than ever, generating an astounding $22 million every day in revenues. Suddenly a new disease called Insufficient Milk Syndrome has been diagnosed, as women increasingly come to believe they aren't capable of producing adequate milk for their baby. Yet, throughout the animal kingdom, it is practically unknown for a mammal in her natural environment to give birth and not produce enough milk for her offspring. In fact many traditional societies that have not abandoned breastfeeding have nearly a hundred percent of mothers successfully nursing their children.

Everywhere I turn, bottle-feeding is encouraged. The seemingly wholesome children's books I borrow from the library show babies drinking from bottles. A picture of a baby bottle is universally recognized as the sign of baby-changing facilities. As new parents, my husband and I were repeatedly encouraged to leave our baby with someone else (necessitating bottle feeding) and go out by ourselves. One synagogue I was in actually asked me to stop breastfeeding in the sanctuary and sent me into the bathroom. (Even though I showed no skin, the authorities considered my behavior immodest.) I had come to the synagogue for my nephew's bar mitzvah, and nursing kept my babbling baby from being disruptive. As requested, I removed my baby from my breast, her vocalizations increased, and out of consideration for others we had to leave. Situations like this push less-committed mothers to switch to the bottle.

Advocating Breastfeeding

Breastfeeding advocates such as myself have become more vocal in recent years and we are experiencing a backlash. Just recently, when I was part of a panel discussion on raising vegan children, someone asked me which I thought was better for a baby—formula based on cow's milk or formula based on soy. I replied that I really couldn't say, but there were serious problems with both. While both are capable of keeping a baby alive, I said, I added that I would never consider them a substitute for mother's milk, rather something to use in extreme circumstances. After the session ended, a women from the audience came up to me, and said very sternly: "I think you need to be sensitized to this issue of bottle-feeding. Sometimes women have no choice. I had to work when my baby was young," she continued. Recognizing that it was obviously a very upsetting topic for her, I told this mother I could appreciate the difficult situation she was in and knew she did what she felt she must. Sometimes in life our choices are between two things that both seem pretty lousy at the time and there are no easy answers. We each must try to figure out what makes the most sense in the context of our own particular situation.

I happen to believe so strongly in the benefits of human breast milk for my babies that if for some reason I really couldn't nurse (if I was on dangerous medication for example), I would probably try to get milk donated from another nursing mother. However, since I haven't really had to travel such a difficult path, I might not be able to pull that off. It is not my intention to judge mothers who don't breastfeed, but rather to make sure they all have accurate information upon which to base their feeding choices. Formula companies, cultural norms, misinformed doctors, friends and family members, and pressure to "keep up materially" all undermine breastfeeding—I am merely trying to balance those forces that influence how families feed their babies. Compassion for the woman and her difficult situation should not deter us from communicating plainly and truthfully to all parents the importance of breastfeeding and the dangers of using anything else in place of mother's milk. The babies deserve our compassion too.

Breastfeeding Successfully

I can almost always predict who will be breastfeeding two months after their babies are born and who will not. It's very simple. I ask the new mother-to-be one question: "Are you planning to breastfeed?" With few exceptions, women who firmly tell me they are and convey a commitment to giving their baby this best possible start are nursing at two months and usually long after that. But almost every time a woman answers me by telling me she's going to try, she fails.

The single most important factor in a mother's success at breastfeeding her baby is her own commitment. This, of course, depends upon exposure to the real facts about infant feeding. I strongly encourage all pregnant women to attend at least four La Leche

League meetings prior to giving birth, even if they don't plan to breastfeed, just so they can make an informed decision. They should also have accurate information about how to nurse, since there's so much more to it than you might at first guess. The second most important factor in breastfeeding success is whether the woman's partner recognizes and wants the benefits of breast milk for their children. John McDougall M.D., author of a number of books on health and the practice of medicine, minces no words when he talks about the importance of breastfeeding—he feels it is practically child abuse to deprive an infant of its mother's milk.

Even adoptive mothers can breastfeed their infants. Using donated breast milk in a little bag the mother wears and a special tube that carries it along her body to her nipple, an unlactating mother can nurse her infant from her own breast and have his or her sucking rewarded with real human milk. Over time, and with enough stimulation, the woman's body will produce additional milk—even if she has never herself gone through a pregnancy!

Why should you go to such lengths to give your baby human milk instead of altered concoctions from cows or soybeans? There are many reasons, not least of which is that mothers' milk is living tissue. Its content is not fixed, but changes from the beginning of a feeding to the end, throughout the day, and throughout babyhood— yet always in tune with your baby's changing needs. When your baby's immune system is challenged by bacteria or a virus, this miraculous substance actually increases in certain protective immune factors that help fight that infection. Human milk contains essential fatty acids (EFAs) not found in formula. EFAs are necessary for development of the brain and retina. Breast milk also contains an extremely absorbable form of iron. (Formula based on cow's milk, however, may irritate the gut, causing a loss of blood and increasing the risk of anemia.) While babies can become sensitized (and allergic) to cow's milk or soymilk, I've never seen evidence of a baby becoming allergic to its mother's milk. (However, a mother who herself consumes dairy can pass molecules of dairy protein to her baby through her own milk and this can sensitize, cause allergies, colic, and possibly even diabetes.)

In fact, if you have a family history of type-one diabetes, a growing body of research suggests that you may be able to prevent it ever affecting your child if you never expose your child to products made from cow's milk. This would mean avoiding all milk, ice cream, butter, whey, casein (a milk protein), cheese, and other dairy products while pregnant and while nursing as well. Apparently, a protein in dairy called BSA can trigger an immune response in genetically susceptible individuals that cross-reacts with cells of the pancreas, destroying them.

Until about four to six months of age, babies' intestines are extremely permeable to large molecules. The permeability allows the antibodies (which are themselves large protein molecules) in mother's milk to be absorbed from the gut directly into the baby's bloodstream. However, this extreme permeability also allows other proteins—if present—to pass into the bloodstream, and these are recognized by the baby's immune system as "foreign" and can be the initiators for allergies. In babies with a genetic susceptibility to allergies, it may be that this period of permeability lasts much longer.

Recently, there has been something of an epidemic of serious allergies to latex. While most experts relate this to the extensive use of latex in surgical gloves and steel-belted radial tires, astonishingly no one seems to connect this to the fact that the nipples on most bottles and pacifiers are also made of latex. Could exposure to latex at a critical point in infancy be sensitizing people and laying the foundation for them to later develop serious allergies to this substance? According to the American Nurses Association, one percent of the general population and eight to twelve percent of all health care workers are allergic to latex. Some of these reactions are quite serious and have resulted in a number of deaths.

Breastfeeding for the Long Term

Although more parents start out breastfeeding than did a few years ago, most don't understand what it means to "fully" breastfeed. While it is certainly better for a baby to get some of its mother's milk than none at all, breast milk and nothing else is absolutely the optimum food for at least the first six months of life. If the baby is being nursed whenever he or she likes, there is actually no need to give anything else for the entire first year. Unlike cats and dogs, who have a very rich milk capable of sustaining their young for periods of time while they go out to hunt, our milk—like that of all primates—is very watery. This kind of milk is best suited to animals who carry their young with them continuously and nurse them frequently all day long. Many nursing babies are quite happy sucking for a few minutes here and there several times each hour. For toddlers, frequently "keeping in touch" with their mother this way gives them the confidence to separate and go exploring on their own later on. I know people whose children were barely interested in eating anything but breast milk until two years, and these children developed and progressed extremely well.

In our family, we have a strong history of allergies and asthma. When our first baby developed eczema after solids were introduced at six months of age (I was a victim of bad information, believing that I had to introduce an iron-fortified rice cereal to prevent anemia), we returned to a diet of total breast milk until about a year and sought the help of a homeopath. The homeopathic remedy cleared the problem right up. Thankfully, at five years of age, our baby is still allergy free. With our second baby we tried to hold off introducing solids as long as possible. At eight months, because she made a tremendous fuss every time the rest of us ate, we caved in and allowed her some steamed veggies with the family at the evening meal. We felt that her need to feel a part of the family dinner now outweighed the benefit to her immune system of postponing solids.

The benefits of breastfeeding extend beyond strengthening the immune system to touch on many different aspects of development. Because a baby must actually work her or his jaw to get milk from the breast, breastfeeding develops the musculature of the face in a way that bottle-feeding does not. This may be a factor in the lower rate of speech and orthodontic problems seen in long-term fully breastfed babies. Because a nursing baby goes from one breast to another during feedings, always close enough to its mother's face to focus on it, the neurological pathways associated with eye develop-ment get the kind of stimulation they need, at just the right time. While it is possible to overfeed a baby on formula, with a totally breastfed baby one can relax and allow one's baby to nurse as much as he or she wants. Since the water content, fat content, and other nutritional parameters of breast milk fluctuate to meet the baby's changing needs (i.e., thirst, hunger, comfort), the baby learns to honor his or her own body's signals.

Breast milk is both a food and a medicine. Every time one of my children developed a runny nose or cough, I would wonder if it might turn into something bad, although so far my fears have been unfounded. When this happens my baby or toddler always wants to nurse more than usual, and I always oblige. It is wonderful to be able to offer my children my milk, and it is very comforting to cuddle up together, knowing that my body is probably developing antibodies and passing them to my child. By nursing, I know I'm doing absolutely the best possible thing for my child.

Because breastfeeding has worked so well and so quickly, we have never felt the need to resort to any pharmaceuticals—with their potential side effects—to cure a problem. While pinkeye and other types of eye infection are common in babies and preschoolers, breast milk has saved us there too! In fact, I've even squirted breast milk in my children's eyes at the first sign of pus or red eyes and it has cleared things right up. It worked just as well in my own eyes when

I developed an eye infection from improper handling of my contact lenses.

Other Reasons Why Breast Is Best

Everyone has heard that mother–infant bonding is one of the great benefits of nursing, but few have considered some of the more profound ramifications. Nursing is far more than sustenance—it is a great source of comfort to a baby or child. I love the fact that my children associate human touch and the milk from my body as their primary sources of comfort. I believe that babies who are encouraged to seek comfort from mother substitutes like bottles or pacifiers will be more inclined as adults to seek comfort in material things rather than people and relationships.

Environmentally, breastfeeding is far superior. There's no litter and no packaging gets dumped in the landfill. No energy is wasted attempting to transform mammary secretions from other animals or the extractions from soybeans into substances that won't outright kill an infant. It is also convenient. At any time or any place, breast milk is the right temperature. There are no worries about lead, plastic, or aluminum from your milk's packaging getting into your baby (something that has been documented as occurring with artificial baby milks many times). There is no hysterical baby screaming while you frantically look for bottles and nipples or warm formula in the middle of the night. Because we've always slept with our babies at night, nursing has become even more convenient.

For mothers, there are additional benefits to nursing. According to *Milk, Money, and Madness*, these include fewer urinary tract infections, a reduced risk of hip fracture and osteoporosis, and lower rates of breast, cervical, and ovarian cancer.

When to Wean

Despite the fact that, worldwide, babies are nursed for an average of 4.2 years, people in the United States assume that even if you start out nursing, you will very soon wean your infant from breast to bottle. But it is worth considering that if your baby still has a need to suck or still has a nutritional need for a high-fat, calorie-dense food (which babies do need until at least two years of age), it would seem illogical to substitute an artificial baby milk for the superior substance. And why, when your child starts playing with others at around two and is suddenly exposed to all sorts of germs, would you want to withdraw the most healing, best sickness preventative there is—breast milk?

When I first started out nursing, I planned to do it for about a year. But when my daughter turned one, it was clear to me that nursing was providing so much for her nutritionally and emotionally that stopping was out of the question. As she became a toddler, nursing was a wonderful way for her to calm down and for us to reconnect after I had intercepted something she felt she had to do, but which I deemed not in her best interest. At about two years of age, we started participating in various different programs with lots of other children and she was exposed to a host of new germs. I couldn't consider withdrawing this marvelous protective substance at that point—especially since, if we did quit and she got sick, I knew I'd have no breast milk to give her. So on we went.

When my first child turned three, my husband and I wanted to have a second child, and I felt I really needed some time to have my body back to myself before embarking on another pregnancy. One month before my older child's third birthday, I started talking to her about not nursing anymore. By this time, the frequency of nursing had dropped off quite a bit and some days she didn't even ask to nurse at all. Every few days we talked a little bit about how wonderful nursing had been and how on her third birthday we would nurse together for the last time. We made the day special, and we said "goodbye" to nursing. She accepted it very well. While she did ask to nurse a few times more after that, she never made much fuss when I offered to hold her and hug her instead. Now she fondly remembers nursing and talks often about how she plans to nurse her babies when she grows up.

Anthropologists who have studied other primates have extrapolated the data from them to try to come up with the "natural age" for weaning in humans. They estimate it to be at around four to seven years of age. Interestingly, until about the age of five, the saliva of most humans contains the enzyme lactase, which allows us to digest the lactose in milk. There must be a reason for this.

Breastfeeding: A Protection against Pollution

With the increasing level of pollution and contamination that is pervasive in our environment and present to some extent in all plants and animals—even those raised organically—many mothers are concerned about how they can reduce the level of pesticides and endocrine-disrupting chemicals in their milk. As we go through life, all animals tend to accumulate these chemicals and store them in their fatty tissue.

One of the few times that we excrete significant amounts is when we lactate. Therefore, it makes sense to eat in a way that generally exposes us to the least amount of chemicals possible. According to a letter printed in *The New England Journal of Medicine* on March 26, 1981, researchers found that the breast milk of women whose diets were composed exclusively of plants had only one to two percent of the level of various chemicals found in the milk of the average American woman. Another study published in 1983 in the Scandinavian medical journal *Acta Paediatr Scand* showed that women who didn't eat meat but drank cow's milk had lower levels of contaminants in their milk than omnivores. Women who consumed a lot of fish had milk that was the most polluted. (This makes sense since the fish humans eat are the final link in the food chain.) Of additional help, but probably not quite as significant, would be to eat as much of our food as possible from organically grown sources.

Breastfeeding provides so much for children physically and emotionally. It strengthens the immune system, improves neurological development, and reduces the risk of a wide range of illnesses, allergies, and diseases. It benefits the mother's health, too. On top of this, breastfeeding is good for the environment. Yet even in light of all these factors occasionally some husbands still question if there is really that much difference between the mother's breast and a bottle. Dr. John McDougall knows what to say to these men: "Which would you rather cuddle up with . . . a latex nipple attached to a plastic bottle or your wife's breast?"

Chapter Four
Vaccination

WHEN I WAS PREGNANT WITH MY FIRSTBORN, A friend asked me whether I was planning to vaccinate my child.

"What do you mean, am I planning to vaccinate?!" I replied incredulously. I'd never even considered it something to think about. "Of course I will vaccinate my child," I told her. "What parent wouldn't?"

My friend, whose formal college education was in the field of dance, proceeded to share a little bit of information with me about the dangers of vaccines both short and long term. In her view, the risks of vaccination outweighed the benefits. I listened politely to what she said, although as a microbiology major partway through a master's in science education, as well as being a former employee of one of the most respected pharmaceutical companies in the world, I was convinced I was seeing firsthand a classic example of the hazards of scientific illiteracy. My friend after all had studied only dance. I had taken microbiology, immunology, microbial physiology, genetics of microorganisms, biology of the cancer cell, genetic engineering, bacteriology, physics, and three semesters of calculus! Several of my professors had written me glowing letters of recommendation. One had even called me one of the brightest four to six students he'd ever known. Nowhere in any of my courses had I ever heard that there might be a down side to vaccination. The story of Edward

Jenner, who developed the smallpox vaccine, was practically a "Genesis" story to my entire field of study. To even question such dogma (not that it ever occurred to me to do so) would have been scientific blasphemy.

One thing my dancer friend said did make sense to me, however. "You ought to just check it out," she said. "You know, before you automatically put that stuff into your baby."

Getting Informed about Vaccination

And so I did. After all, no matter how minor, common, and assuredly safe it was, it was a medical procedure. A foreign agent would be going into my baby's body. As a parent, I was entrusted with the care of this new being and I owed it to her to gather the best information I could. If I did this, I could put the issue to rest once and for all.

There was not a shred of doubt in my mind. My friend, well-meaning though she was, was scientifically illiterate. Scientific illiteracy had been much talked about in my classes. It was a threat to the best interests of society and here was a prime example. I knew absolutely that vaccines were most certainly modern medicine's biggest success story.

The literature that was easiest to find on the subject came from our local health department, and it was everything I then believed true about vaccines. For the first time ever, however, I paid attention to the fine print that described the adverse reactions—fine print I'd never really looked closely at before. I noticed that there were certainly an awful lot of different types of reaction reported, although I completely dismissed those by reminding myself that the odds of them happening were extremely small.

Next I found a copy of Neil Miller's book *Vaccines: Are They Really Safe and Effective?* While I know many parents who stand by this book, I initially dismissed it. When I looked at the graphs he used to illustrate his points, I found other ways to explain his data that did not necessarily substantiate his view. Here too, in the manipulation of data, was, I thought, another example of scientific illiteracy. However, two of Miller's ideas stuck with me. First was the fact that the incidence of most diseases was sharply declining prior to the introduction of a vaccine. Second, Miller noted that, since the introduction and widespread use of vaccines, the incidence of a variety of autoimmune diseases and learning disorders had increased. Amazingly, despite the fundamental tenet of the Hippocratic oath being "First: Do no harm," there hasn't been a single study I've found that tries to show that vaccines are not linked with the development of cancer, leukemia, multiple sclerosis, lupus, asthma, or autism. These conditions, plus many others, have all been on the rise since the introduction of vaccines. While I am not saying that vaccines cause these things, I am shocked that there are no data that show vaccines are safe, long term. It seems to me that, if society is going to try to force all parents to have their child injected with a biological agent, then we should certainly have data that show that five, ten, or twenty years in the future these vaccines do not wreak havoc with the immune system.

Now my interest was really piqued. With the birth of our first-born, my husband and I agreed that we'd postpone all vaccines while I began to seriously search out everything I could on the topic. I read *A Shot in the Dark* by Harris Coulter and Barbara Loe Fisher and became terrified of the pertussis vaccine. The book vividly describes individual cases where the vaccine led to brain damage or death. As if that wasn't bad enough, the parents' agony was compounded by a medical system that refused to believe the vaccine did this to their children. Then I read accounts of what pertussis was like and became equally terrified of the disease! Also known as whooping cough or the hundred-day cough, it is characterized by coughing episodes so violent that victims sometimes vomit, break ribs, or even suffer asphyxia.

When you question vaccination, most people counter by raising the issue of polio, which still exists in some parts of the globe.

Members of my family who lived through the infamous epidemics of the 1940s and 1950s relayed fearful firsthand accounts of what it was like to live through this time. These seemed compelling reasons to get this vaccine. But then I found out that, since the 1970s, it is the vaccine itself that has caused the majority of the cases of polio acquired in the United States and is responsible for paralyzing about ten citizens each year.

I read magazine articles and books on the subject of vaccination. I talked with everyone I could. I called my old college professors repeatedly to check out various facts. I spent hours on the phone with researchers from the Centers for Disease Control (CDC). I spoke with parents who had opted not to vaccinate. Most of the information on both sides was highly emotional and I wanted facts. Facts, it seemed, without all the hype were hard to come by.

Talking to Specialists

Each time I called the specialists at the CDC, I specifically asked to speak with someone knowledgeable about vaccines. Over the course of multiple phone calls, I spoke with several different researchers. I was shocked to discover they were not familiar with some of the basic history of vaccine problems I'd found detailed in books I had checked out from the local hospital's medical library. As you can imagine, we had many lively debates.

The general view of the CDC specialists was that vaccines were practically risk-free and the diseases they (supposedly) prevented generally disastrous. I remember one conversation in which I expressed concern over vaccine preparations possibly being contaminated with other animal viruses. The scientist I spoke with told me this was ridiculous. I pointed out how it was documented in the medical literature that early batches of polio vaccines were found to have been contaminated with a virus called SV-40, and that many people were injected with this contaminated vaccine. (SV-40 is normally found in monkeys and is frequently used by researchers to turn normal cells into cancer cells.)

The researcher sounded exasperated and questioned where I was getting such bizarre misinformation. He opened a huge reference book of his own to show me how wrong I was. I listened as he read through the section detailing the history of the polio vaccine. His words began to slow down, and I listened while he confirmed exactly what I had said. Although he spoke to me more respectfully after that, I could tell that he gave no more credibility to anything else I said, and I had absolutely no impact on his unwaveringly positive view of vaccines in general. (A question has recently been raised as to whether the virus that causes AIDS was initially another contaminant of early polio vaccines. Apparently a vial containing one of these early vaccine preparations is still stored in a deep freeze and some scientists are demanding that it be tested. I predict we will be hearing more on this topic.)

In our continuing discussion of the merits of vaccination a former microbiology professor whom I admired highly signed a letter to me in the following way: "Dr.——— (Who carries SV-40 because of the Salk vaccine, but who likely is alive only because the Salk vaccine allowed him to survive a vicious polio epidemic)." I find amazing his willingness to dismiss any risk of vaccination while giving it full credit for saving him from this disease—especially when the CDC themselves confirmed that over ninety-nine percent of people exposed to polio never show any symptoms. His assertion that this vaccine saved him from paralysis simply is not supportable by the facts.

Visiting Dr. Scheibner

It made no sense to me to look at risks versus benefits of vaccines on a worldwide basis. In our case, we lived in the United States rather than a developing country. We had good sanitation and our baby was being exclusively breastfed. Our diets were good and there were no raging epidemics (for which vaccines were available) pounding at our door. In the context of our particular lifestyle, what would be best for our baby?

When our firstborn baby was ten months old, my husband and I had the opportunity to go to Australia, where we would be staying in Sydney. I remembered reading about a researcher who lived outside Sydney and who had data linking vaccines with sudden infant death syndrome (SIDS). I dug through my growing pile of papers on the subject until I found her name—Viera Scheibner Ph.D.—and placed her name in my wallet. Once we were settled in Australia, it only took a few phone calls to locate her. I was very hopeful we might see her and perhaps be able to put into perspective the relative risks both for and against vaccination and figure out what would really be best for our baby. We were in luck and got an invitation to her home.

That visit was an eye-opener. Dr. Scheibner brought us into her office, which was a small room lined with file cabinets four drawers tall. Drawer after drawer was filled with reprints of articles from medical journals, all somehow related to the topic of vaccination. Some of the papers dated back to the early 1900s. Dr. Scheibner told us that she had started collecting the papers after data from an infant breathing monitor her husband had designed started signaling alarms at regular, predictable times following routine vaccinations. Her own children, now grown, had been vaccinated, and she had always believed vaccines to be safe and effective. It wasn't until she and her husband began trying to figure out what might be causing SIDS (commonly known as "cot death") that they became suspicious of vaccines. Now, after collecting hundreds of thousands of pages of medical journal articles on the subject, she was convinced that vaccines were neither safe nor effective.

We talked for about three hours. It was an incredible experience to be listened to seriously and actually get some real facts. Dr. Scheibner had an extraordinary recall of the journal articles, and could effectively rebut everything I'd read in the health department's literature on vaccinations. She poked holes in what the CDC's own researchers had told me. She could take a journal article that seemed to prove a vaccination worked and show me how the researchers had dismissed data they considered irrelevant, but which, when included, made their case weak.

One of her arguments that brought into question most of the research that supposedly proves vaccine efficacy was that when vaccine trials are done the test administrators never have a true control group. Dr. Scheibner told me that a true control group would consist of children who have not received any vaccines. However, instead of these, researchers determined that an adequate control group consisted of children who, while they may not have had the vaccine that was being tested, were still being injected with a host of *other* vaccines. Dr. Scheibner believed there were sufficient data to suggest that vaccines in general depress immune function and may make one more likely to get opportunistic infections.

To illustrate, she pointed out that the bacterium that causes some forms of meningitis (*Haemophilus influenzae* B) is generally a harmless organism that normally lives in harmony with a healthy individual. She said that it was increasingly being identified as causing meningitis, a result of our assaulting the immune system with a slew of other vaccines. She described the medical journal article that was used to justify the effectiveness of this vaccine. Although the paper showed that the incidence of what they defined as HIB disease decreased from twenty-two cases in the control group to one case in the vaccine group (there were over four thousand participants in the study), the total number of deaths and hospitalizations between the two groups was essentially the same. Indeed, the total incidence of invasive infections was actually slightly higher in the group receiving the new vaccine.

Dr. Scheibner sounded compelling, but still I was not completely convinced it was true. Could what she was saying be an accurate reading of the journal articles? How would I be able to remember everything she was telling me so I could double-check her facts? While I was thinking these things, Dr. Scheibner showed me her book *Vaccination: 100 Years of Orthodox Research Shows That Vaccines*

Represent a Medical Assault on the Immune System. To this day, *Vaccination* is by far and away the very best book I have read on the topic. It covers all the routine vaccines that were in use in 1993 (the year it was published) and everything she says is referenced to peer-reviewed medical journals. Finally, we had some facts upon which to base our decision.

When we returned to the United States and I had had a chance to digest Dr. Scheibner's book, I began to doubt what she was saying. How come my doctor wasn't aware of these studies? I asked myself. What about the CDC—surely its experts who were pushing vaccines should have seen these studies? Maybe Dr. Scheibner misunderstood what the papers were saying. Maybe she was lying. Maybe the facts in her book just weren't true.

I went to the medical library at the local hospital—many times. Using the references plainly provided in *Vaccination*, I started digging up old journal articles and reading them. It was slow going, as the reading was the most technical I'd encountered since leaving the pharmaceutical industry two years earlier. But I had to know the truth. As it turned out, Dr. Scheibner, apart from a few small inaccuracies and a few leaps of logic I couldn't follow at the time, turned out to be pretty accurate. These leaps of logic were explained to my full satisfaction by Dr. Scheibner on her later visit to the United States.

Our Decision about Vaccinations

That did it for my husband and me. What I continually find amazing about this whole experience is that even though I have spent many hundreds of hours researching vaccination, I and other parents like me (who have made informed choices not to vaccinate) are depicted by the "authorities" as lazy, negligent, or uneducated—indeed, perhaps scientifically illiterate! We have been challenged by dozens of family members, friends, nurses, and even my old professors for making what they all consider an unwise choice. Some have even condemned us for placing others at risk by not vaccinating our children.

Yet many of these people don't have a science background and *none* of them has taken the time to go to the medical library and actually read and digest the primary literature for themselves. This shows you how most people accept the efficacy of vaccination on faith, without ever examining the facts closely.

Of course, I realize that even if they were to examine the situation, some people might still come to a different conclusion than my husband and I regarding the wisdom of vaccination. The fact is, there are no guarantees when it comes to parenthood. As a parent we want more than anything to protect our children from harm and consequently we do the best we can. I think many parents and doctors *want* to believe that modern medicine can offer them something that will keep children safe. While some cultures put their faith in charms and harmless rituals, we put ours in biologically active agents administered by our culture's high priests, the doctors. It's common in this day and age to view technology with awe and belittle what we do naturally. Our doctors' arrogance lies in their belief that what we create is superior to the system that nature evolved—something that the last chapter on bottle-feeding should have made plain is not always true. I find it interesting that companies such as American Home Products and Abbot Laboratories (among perhaps others) make *both* infant formula and vaccines.

There Are No Guarantees
I have said and cannot emphasize enough that there are no guarantees. The doctors can't guarantee you a healthy child if you do vaccinate and the natural health advocates can't guarantee your child's health if you don't. Life is full of risks. I think to some extent a person's view on vaccination is likely to parallel his or her overall worldview. Those who look to technology to solve all problems will probably favor vaccines. Some of us, however, think the system the Creator put into place has more wisdom than our small efforts.

During the course of human evolution, or for that matter the evolution of mammals, our bodies have evolved a system for dealing with assaults by bacteria and viruses. In general, germs gain access to our bodies via the mouth, nose, or eyes, and the immune system begins to fight the disease agent. Next the organism travels to the lymphatic system, where more of the immune system is activated. By the time the bacteria or virus gain access to the bloodstream and major organs, a whole cascade of events have taken place, and many different branches of the immune response have been mobilized. In most cases the disease is fully eliminated from the body.

Let's compare this natural process with what happens when we're injected with a vaccine. The mucous membranes and lymphatic system are completely bypassed and the organism has immediate access to the blood and major organs. No gradual buildup of the immune response has occurred and parts of the immune system have been completely evaded. Could this scenario create a persistent infection at the sub-cellular level, one that the body can never fully rid itself of? It seems reasonable to me that antigens from live virus vaccines could in fact be harbored on cells inside our body, provoking a continuous immune response that in some individuals may lead to autoimmune disease—in other words, attacks by their immune system on their very own cells.

Given our situation, my husband and I felt we would rather put our faith in doing all that we could to build up our children's immune systems and work with nature, rather than avoid millions of years of evolution and risk assaulting our child's immune system for disease risks that presently are remote.

Why We Said No to Vaccination

So just what were these facts we discovered that were so compelling? In the interest of keeping things brief, I will touch on only a few.[1] Let's start with polio—the disease that strikes more fear in everyone than any of the others. Despite all the horror stories we've all heard, it is worth considering this: According to the section on polio in the *Merck Manual* (a resource guide well-respected by the entire medical community): "Inapparent infections (the main source of spread) are common in unimmunized populations, but overt disease is rare except during epidemics; even then, the ratio of unapparent infections to clinical cases exceeds 100:1." What this means to you or me is that in a worst case scenario, over ninety-nine percent of those exposed to the wild polio virus will be just fine.

So how do you explain the experience of those who lived through the epidemic and say it was awful? Partly, I think hysteria made it seem worse than it was. But also, prior to the introduction of the Salk vaccine, the diagnosis of the disease was based on any paralysis lasting more than twenty-four hours. This diagnosis could have included cases of aseptic meningitis, muscular dystrophy, and Guillain-Barré syndrome. After the vaccine was in use, diagnosis was confirmed by the presence of the virus. This alone would have shown a decrease in the incidence of the disease whether the vaccine worked or not.

But there's more. The medical journals indicate there are two things that make one more likely to develop paralysis when exposed to the polio virus. The first is any intramuscular injection within thirty days of incubating the polio virus.[2] The second is having one's tonsils removed. It turns out that the operation du jour during the polio epidemic was the tonsillectomy, and the whole epidemic came right on the heels of the first mass diphtheria vaccinations. In his book *Vaccines: Are They Really Safe and Effective?* Neil Miller describes how one doctor, Benjamin Sandler, linked polio paralysis with consumption of refined sugar and actually convinced people in his area to reduce their consumption of soda pop and ice cream. This resulted in a temporary decrease in polio in this geographic area, a decrease that lasted until those who sold these products convinced consumers it was a myth. When consumption resumed, so did incidents of polio.

Those facts certainly put polio in a different light. Critics of the above points might rightly argue that, since the polio vaccine can be taken orally, it mimics the way one would normally contact this disease—in which case, why not just take it? Well, it turns out that polio, like all viruses, cannot simply be grown in culture media, but must be grown on live cells. In the case of polio, the cells used to cultivate it are from monkey kidney tissue. Monkeys harbor all sorts of bacteria and viruses. Because we are so similar to monkeys from a physiological perspective, whatever can infect them can also probably infect us. However, because human and monkey populations generally have little contact, we have little natural immunity to monkey diseases. A minor monkey illness could, therefore, be life threatening for a human. In fact, as I mentioned earlier, medical history books confirm that some preparations of polio vaccine have been contaminated with monkey viruses, and we can screen batches of polio vaccine for known viruses (like SV-40 mentioned earlier). Unfortunately we can't screen for contaminating viruses that we haven't yet identified.

Whooping Cough

Pertussis, or whooping cough, has received the most press for the potential dangers of the vaccine that is supposed to prevent it. As I suggested before, questions have been raised as to whether this vaccine is linked with SIDS, asthma, convulsions, and other brain disorders.

What most people don't know, however, is that the orthodox medical literature shows that the vaccine offers little in the way of protection. There is good documentation of outbreaks occurring in fully vaccinated populations of all ages. Furthermore, several studies suggest that, regardless of vaccination status, pertussis is endemic in the population and only in young babies does it present us with the classic severe symptoms. In fact, one study, at the University of California, Los Angeles[3] showed that during a thirty-month period, twenty-six percent of students going to the school health service with complaints of a cough lasting at least six days actually had whooping cough (and most of these students had been fully vaccinated).

After learning this, my husband and I figured the best way to protect our babies was to keep them at home and out of public places for the first couple of months, and then when going out not to let anyone with a cold or strangers get close. After our babies reached one year, we figured that they were mature enough to survive pertussis and we relaxed a bit.

Essentially we have looked at every single vaccine currently recommended for children, and, with each, we have found compelling reasons to avoid it. With respect to measles, mumps, rubella, and chickenpox, we hope to expose our children to these illnesses sometime between their third and ninth birthdays, when the illness is typically the most mild and complications least likely. Recovery then generally leads to lifelong immunity.

One concern with the vaccines for these illnesses is that immunity from the vaccine can wear off and leave one vulnerable to the disease as an adult, when the risks of complications are greater. In fact, in recent years, the media have covered epidemics of measles occurring in college students who were vaccinated as children. Prior to routine vaccination, epidemics in this age group were unheard of. In our reading we have found evidence that good nutrition can lessen the seriousness of all of these infections. Adequate vitamin A is supposed to be important in reducing complications of measles.

Tetanus

The one vaccine I still wonder about is tetanus. Many people I know who have opted not to vaccinate their children have made an exception for this one. However, it is my understanding that the single most important factor in preventing a tetanus infection is good wound management. If not having the tetanus vaccine really does put one at serious risk, then wouldn't we be hearing about how the children of Christian Scientists (a group that largely eschews all vaccines) had a significant risk of tetanus?

But for me the most compelling evidence for not getting this vaccine for my children is my own personal experience. Years ago, before I was married, I spent six months traveling around Australia, New Zealand, and Fiji. During this time, some nurses I met convinced me to get a tetanus booster shot, since I couldn't remember when my last one had been. Later that trip, I developed a raging yeast infection. It was so bad that the doctors I went to misdiagnosed it at first and none of the medications adequately controlled it. Nothing like this had ever happened to me before and it took about six weeks before it cleared up.

I would never ever have linked these two events together if it were not for a paper I happened to come across many years later. This paper quoted a study in *The New England Journal of Medicine*[4] that said that a temporary AIDS-like state can be induced in patients following tetanus vaccination. This study found a reduction in the ratio of T-helper to T-suppressor cells. The largest drop occurred between three and fourteen days post vaccination.

This came as a revelation to me. One of the best-known symptoms of AIDS was yeast infection, and I began to wonder: Is overgrowth of yeast a result of depression of T-cell populations? I thought back to my own experience. Both the tetanus vaccine and the horrendous yeast infection occurred while I was in New Zealand, but I wondered whether the vaccine could have caused my infection. Although it was a long time ago and I simply could not remember more specifics about the timing of each, I fortunately had kept a journal throughout my trip. I dug it out and read through it and, amazingly, exactly two weeks after I received the vaccine the yeast infection had started!

I shared this startling discovery with a friend of mine who works in a research lab, and she shared a similar experience with me. She told me about a coworker who had recently gone to give blood as she had routinely done for years and was told that her blood showed that she was in the late stages of an AIDS infection and that they couldn't use it. This woman had absolutely no risk factors for AIDS and was shocked. To her relief, extensive follow-up medical tests then revealed that this first test was in error. The two women (my friend and her coworker) had racked their brains trying to explain what had happened. The only thing that kept coming to mind was that this woman had gotten a tetanus shot several weeks prior to donating the blood.

To me, all this strongly suggests that tetanus shots depress the immune system, at least temporarily. Every time I start to worry what would happen if my child steps on a rusty nail, I remember my own experience. I'd rather gamble doing things to strengthen my children's immune systems rather than attack them.

Several months ago a friend of mine's five-year-old boy, who has never been vaccinated, stepped on a huge metal rod at a construction site where a very old house had just been torn down. It made a deep puncture wound in his foot. His parents took him immediately to the emergency room, where they thoroughly scrubbed out the wound and stitched it up. For several weeks the parents treated him homeopathically and with vitamin C. They worried about whether he would be all right. He has had no problems.

Your Decision about Vaccination
Unfortunately, most parents don't know they actually have a choice about whether to vaccinate or not. Multinational drug companies come up with these products to sell, doctors make money administering them, and both organizations work together to get laws passed requiring proof of vaccination for admission to public school. What capitalist couldn't see the potential in this?

Although laws vary by state, it is possible to call your local health department and ask for the statute numbers specifying your state's legal requirements regarding vaccination. You can take this information to your local library and the librarian can help you find out what the law actually says. In general, all states allow exemptions from vaccinations for medical reasons, such as if your child is allergic to vaccine components, has already had a severe reaction to a previous vaccine, or if an older sibling has. However, a medical exemption requires a doctor to write a note on your behalf.

Some states allow a philosophical exemption, which would be the easiest for parents to use, and simply requires you to state in writing that you choose not to vaccinate for philosophical reasons. Most states also allow a religious exemption. According to an attorney I heard speaking on this issue, the Supreme Court, when addressing the issue of religious freedom, has said that any belief one holds as dearly as one would hold a religious belief qualifies as a religious belief and is protected by law. Furthermore, the state does not have the right to inquire as to what one's religion is, or to request the name of one's priest, rabbi, minister, etc., to vouch for that person's religious belief.

Some families I know have circumvented the vaccination requirement by using the religious exemption. Others home-school and so haven't had to deal with it. Some parents have actually falsified their vaccination records rather than deal with this intrusion. Whatever you decide to do, however, take the time to look into the issue carefully—the consequences could be serious either way. If something bad does happen to your child, you can at least know that you took the time to make an informed decision, and did the best you could with the information available. As parents, we cannot expect any more or less of ourselves.

---

1. For a more thorough discussion by a medical doctor about the dangers of some of the vaccines I am skipping, I would recommend the classic book by Robert Mendelsohn M.D., entitled *How to Raise a Healthy Child in Spite of Your Pediatrician*. In Dr. Mendelsohn's book there is a section that specifically addresses vaccination. I remember reading an early version of this book that discussed the dangers of the tetanus vaccine; however, the edition I now own, published in 1984 by Ballantine Books, has mysteriously omitted this part.
2. *New England Journal of Medicine*, Feb. 23, 1995.
3. *Clinical Infectious Diseases*, Oct. 1995.
4. Nov. 26, 1981, p. 1307.

Chapter Five
Vegan Children

W E ALL WANT OUR CHILDREN TO HAVE A GOOD life and good health. Since the two are linked, our task as parents should be to make choices that give our children the best chances of having a good, healthy life. Most parents seem to place more emphasis upon how well their children treat others rather than how they care for themselves. But *both* are important. *Both* are critical to having a balanced, well-adjusted self.

What Being a Vegan Means

I am a vegan and I am raising my children as vegans. This means that neither my children nor I eat any animal products. I believe this diet represents an excellent way of maintaining my health, the health of my children, and the health of the planet and the animals who share it with us. There have been innumerable studies that show that a vegetarian—or better yet, a vegan—diet lowers the risk of heart disease and can even reverse its effects. The diet has been shown to be effective in preventing several forms of cancer. For instance, a twelve-year study published in the *British Medical Journal* in 1994 showed that lacto-ovo vegetarians had a forty-percent lower death rate then omnivores.

This chapter aims to show that a vegan diet is not only possible but desirable for your children. I believe that raising a child to want and enjoy the standard American diet—which is high in fat, low in fiber, and nutritionally poor—is like providing them with a lifelong ball and chain. Why do we raise our children to eat in a way that practically assures that they will develop some chronic degenerative disease?

The Deed Shapes the Heart

There's a saying in Judaism: "The deed shapes the heart." By modeling a vegan lifestyle for my children, while explaining why and how we are eating the way we are, I am building a framework for moral behavior. Three or more times a day, my children participate in an activity (eating) that is laying the foundation for how to live a life that is considerate towards others, respectful of the environment, and caring for oneself.

Eating is the one activity we do daily that has the potential not only to impact our own personal health, but to touch the lives of every other being on this planet. Howard Lyman, who turned from being a fourth-generation cattle rancher into an advocate for veganism, understands the impact of our eating habits. He says: "The most dangerous weapon in the human arsenal is the fork."

Too much of today's scientific research is focused upon finding the genetic basis for cancer, heart disease, and myriad other fatal and crippling illnesses, distracting people from the simple but profound fact that the environment is often the most critical factor in whether one's genetic predispositions are realized. Our internal environment is created by the food, air, and water we take into our bodies while our external environment is being degraded because of the waste and pollution caused directly or indirectly by intensive, animal-based agriculture.

A vegan diet consists exclusively of the consumption of four particular food groups: fruits, vegetables, grains, and legumes. It includes every food that can be prepared entirely from things of plant origin. Food such as meat, fish, dairy, and eggs, and ingredients and byproducts derived from animals (such as gelatin), are *not* part of a vegan diet. Being vegan, however, extends beyond not eating animal products. It involves looking at one's entire lifestyle and working to make choices based upon compassion. A vegan looks at what she buys, what she wears, the cleaning products she uses, and much more with an eye to making choices that don't support the exploitation of people or destruction of the environment, cause poor health or harm animals.

My husband and I were both raised on a meat-and-dairy–centered diet and enjoyed eating all the traditional American foods. We had grown up considering ourselves animal lovers. However, it wasn't until I was thirteen that I ever considered the hypocrisy of "loving" animals in general and then sitting down to a meal and eating the body of one. My husband didn't make this connection until he met me.

Lowering My Cholesterol

I was an adolescent when my family got a farm and started raising beef cattle on it. When the calves born on our farm matured enough to be taken away from their mothers to be fattened for slaughter, I realized that the baby cows I had watched and loved could end up on my plate. As the calves were loaded into trucks and carted away, their mothers stood at the fence and cried out desperately. They remained in the area where they had last seen their babies for three days, bellowing their sad cries. My father later told me that standing watching those mothers crying out made him feel like an SS agent at Auschwitz. Although it took another twenty-five years and the threat of a heart attack for him to stop eating cows, that scene put an end to his cattle-ranching days.

I, on the other hand, changed my diet immediately—vowing never again to eat another cow. But it took much longer for my feelings of compassion to extend beyond mammals to birds and fish. I had a great deal of attachment to eating them! Although I thought of myself as a vegetarian, all I had really done was to stop eating red meat and for the most part birds. However, even this small change significantly affected my health. I'd always been a chubby child—and for the first time I started to slim down. When my parents took me on a trip to Israel with a group of about forty others, I was the only one who didn't eat mammals and birds and the only one who didn't get sick. It was a foreshadowing of the power that making conscious food choices has.

Records of my total cholesterol level show that it was 190 after I cut out red meat—too high for a teenager. (I have no idea how much higher it might have been before that.) By the end of high school I had almost completely stopped eating animal flesh (although I still ate lots of dairy and eggs), and there was still no change. By graduate school, I was no longer eating eggs, and my cholesterol dropped to 163. At the age of thirty, after I had eliminated all animal products from my diet, my cholesterol level had dropped to 144, with an HDL (good cholesterol) of 49.3 (usually cholesterol levels increase as we age).

The China Study, an ongoing population study started in 1983 and jointly sponsored by Cornell, Oxford, and Beijing universities, is the largest, most comprehensive study ever to examine diet and lifestyle factors as they relate to risk from disease. Rural China was selected for this study because the diets there vary by province and the people in a particular area tend to eat the same thing as their ancestors. Consequently, it's an ideal living laboratory. In one province people on an average diet may derive ten percent of their calories from animal products; in another province, they may derive eight percent; in a third, it might be five percent, and so forth.

The study compared data on 6,500 Chinese citizens living in sixty-five different provinces. T. Colin Campbell, the primary author of this study, found that one's total cholesterol level was the single best predictor of an individual's risk of a variety of degenerative diseases. The study also found that cholesterol levels were closely linked with the quantity of animal protein in the diet. Results of the China

Study strongly suggest that the nearer a person's diet comes to being entirely plant-based, the lower the individual's risk of heart disease and a variety of cancers.

Part of the benefit from a plant-based diet is due to what isn't in it—hormones, antibiotics, saturated fat, cholesterol, animal protein, and several infectious diseases associated with animal flesh and milk. Virgil Hulse, a former dairy inspector for the state of California, wrote a book entitled *Mad Cows and Milk Gate*, in which he explains how diseased animals are producing a lot of the food we all assume is safe. Hulse states that over sixty percent of all dairy herds are infected with bovine leukemia virus. Since milk from a number of different herds gets pooled during transport and processing, the chances are good that anyone regularly consuming dairy products is being exposed to a variety of pathogenic organisms, since pasteurization does not kill everything. Hulse also discusses the possibility that some of the diseases prevalent in dairy cows might be causing sickness in humans as well

The Centers for Disease Control estimate that there are between six million and eighty million cases of food-borne illness in the United States each year. Symptoms of these diseases include diarrhea, vomiting, paralysis, arthritis, localized infections, and death. The CDC estimate around nine thousand people die annually as a direct result of unsafe food. Setting aside the cost in human health and lives, the economic toll alone is enormous. Illness caused by salmonella alone is thought to cost us one billion dollars a year in medical costs and lost wages, and it is just one of 250 different food-borne illnesses that have been described. Meat, dairy, and eggs are overwhelmingly the primary sources of food-borne illnesses— although the incidence of infections from fruits and vegetables is increasing due to the use of contaminated animal feces as fertilizer, or unsanitary conditions during transport. By purchasing fruits and vegetables whole and washing them before cutting into them, one can virtually eliminate this risk. Even washing and cooking animal foods doesn't always eliminate the risk of consuming harmful organisms, which are often found contaminating the interior of the food as well.

Generational Health Problems

One very disturbing factor in our current dietary system is that the effects of the Standard American Diet (SAD) manifest themselves to a greater degree in each successive generation. A recently published book, *Life in the Womb*, explains how a pregnant mother's diet could not only impact her offspring's lifetime risk for various diseases, but may have consequences for her grandchildren as well. The oldest people alive today were most likely breastfed as babies, and during their formative years were less likely to eat anything as contrived as a TV dinner or fast food. The many artificial colors, sweeteners, and flavors common in today's processed food were not so prevalent in the food chain fifty or sixty years ago. And while some harmful, trans-fatty acids (also known as hydrogenated fat) can be created by normal cooking processes, most people half a century ago didn't have access to foods that contained them in such large amounts. In addition, the food grown then didn't have the disadvantage of being contaminated by agricultural chemicals that became used by farmers in the decades immediately after World War II.

Let's now compare the oldest living generation to their grandchildren and great-grandchildren. In spite of all the medical technology that is supposed to be increasing the quality of life for these subsequent generations, the reality is that asthma is epidemic, antibiotic use is pervasive, childhood leukemia and cancers are on the rise, learning disabilities, attention deficit disorders, autism, and autoimmune disorders are increasing. Why is this the case?

I believe that most health problems today will in the near future be indisputably linked with exposure to a wide variety of environmental toxins—in food, water, air, or medications. In addition, our failure to consume food that is good for us—fresh fruits and vegetables—will also be seen as a contributing factor. Unfortunately, there is so much invested in the current dysfunctional agribusiness, pharmaceutical, and petrochemical industries—as well as so much power wielded by them—that change will be extremely difficult. In her book *Tainted Truth, Wall Street Journal* editor Cynthia Crossen documents the way corporations and special interests influence the outcomes of studies and polls while financing them. Ultimately, these results sway the media and professionals, who then shape public opinion. This makes it very difficult for the public to know that things are wrong, and even more difficult for things to change. Because of this, it is vital for parents to educate themselves in order to protect their children, rather than waiting for regulatory agencies or health care professionals to do something.

Removing Toxins from Your Diet

One benefit of eating a plant-based diet is that data suggest that as one moves up the food chain, there is an accumulation of whatever toxins exist in the environment. By eating only foods of plant origin, you minimize your exposure to pesticides and pollution. When you consume meat, you eat that animal's lifetime exposure to chemicals, which they themselves accumulate and store in their body. Fish tend to be the most contaminated, because humans eat the big fish at the top of the food chain—they ingest the environmental pollutants in the ocean and those gathered by the smaller animal life they themselves eat. One of the times that an animal excretes these toxins is during lactation. So products made from cow's or goat's milk are likely to be more polluted than plant foods.

There is an argument, articulated by scientist Bruce Ames, that synthetic chemicals are not problematic. He feels that, because there are so many hundreds of thousands of toxic chemicals naturally present in plants, the few thousands of synthetic ones we have made are minor by comparison. Ames points out that the plants we eat contain some naturally occurring substances that are very highly toxic, but that our bodies have evolved a system for denaturing and excreting these compounds. Therefore, he argues, our bodies can handle the synthetic chemicals too.

I disagree with this line of thinking. Any substances naturally occurring in plants we eat are things we've likely had hundreds of thousands of years to adapt to. The liver is a highly specialized organ capable of synthesizing a wide variety of enzymes whose function is to break down and detoxify many of the substances found naturally in our foods. Synthetic chemicals, such as DDT and PCBs, however, are not broken down and excreted. That's why we find them concentrated in the fat tissue of virtually every animal on the planet that's been studied. One hundred years ago DDT (and hundreds of other chemicals common today in human bodies) couldn't be found in any animal's tissue. Because the enzymes present in plants and animals do not detoxify many synthetic compounds, these compounds persist, and normal biological processes don't degrade them into harmless substances the way they would naturally occurring toxins. So, while nature does indeed recycle, she hasn't figured out an efficient way to deal with all these new chemicals humans have created.

While humans keep making synthetic toxins, their concentrations grow in the environment. Because they are ubiquitous, eating plants means you take some in. Even organic foods, although considerably cleaner, are likely to contain some synthetic chemicals. If you eat animals, however, then you're eating the animal's lifetime exposure to these chemicals. It is, therefore, important to feed your children only plant foods if you want to reduce their exposure to environmental toxins.

So what exactly is the danger of these synthetic chemicals? According to a fascinating book, *Our Stolen Future* by scientist Theo Colborn, many of these chemicals are capable of hormone disruption—that is, they mimic or interfere with the effect of natural hormones in our body. Since hormones are essentially the messengers for a wide array of activities in our body, and can influence the expression

of genes, anything that interferes with them can have dramatic consequences—especially if exposure occurs before birth or in infancy.
Reproduction, immune system function, even mood are all impacted
by hormones. There is also evidence that some consequences, while
not obvious now, will potentially rise in future generations.

Colborn makes a compelling case that hormone disrupters can
wreak havoc in biological systems in concentrations as low as parts
per trillion. Furthermore, she shares evidence that these chemicals
could be in almost anything made from synthetic chemicals, including plastics. After reading her book, I've made a concerted effort to
minimize contact of my family's food and drink with all kinds of
plastic—especially if the food is hot or acidic. I give my baby unfin-
ished wooden toys to teethe on, rather than plastic. When pregnant,
I was even more careful. Since the impact of hormone disrupters
appears to be more related to timing than concentration, prenatal
exposure at certain developmental times could have significant
impacts, while a short time later the impact might be zero. This fact
is part of the reason we've had such difficulty deciphering the impact
of many chemicals now in use. The old system of testing high doses
and looking at carcinogenicity misses some of the most alarming
consequences of synthetic chemicals.

Getting Positive about Your Health
Let's now accentuate the positive, and look at what positive things
we can do about our health. Joel Fuhrman M.D. is well-known in
the natural hygiene movement and the author of *Fasting and Eating
for Health*. Dr. Fuhrman has a formula for looking at what the
healthiest foods for humans are. He says that the only thing we
know that really extends our life span is calorie restriction. However,
one must still get sufficient nutrients.

The nutrients Dr. Fuhrman is referring to are not just proteins,
fats, carbohydrates, vitamins, and minerals, but also a wide variety
(thousands) of phytochemicals and fibers found only in plant foods.

Dr. Fuhrman says that we have to consider the nutrients per calorie consumed (N/C) of the different foods in our diet and work to maximize our intake of nutrients while keeping calories to a minimum. As we look at the whole range of foods we could eat, those with the highest N/C are raw leafy greens followed by other vegetables, followed by legumes. At the very bottom of his chart are those foods high in calories but offering little in the way of nutrition. As you might imagine, these are foods of animal origin—meat, dairy, and eggs.

I raise my children on a vegan diet because I believe it gives them the best odds of being healthy over the long term and having a good quality of life. But I also raise them vegan because I believe it starts them on the path to make moral choices. I do not want my children to grow up unaware of the suffering or exploitation of nonhuman animals, just as I would think it morally wrong for them to be unaware of the exploitation of slaves or the degradation of women.

Now that the messages of the civil rights and women's rights movements have become part of the tapestry of our culture, most people today find it incredible that people who saw themselves as striving to live just and moral lives could have denied the rights of these two disenfranchised groups. There has been an enormous amount of work over the last thirty years on animal rights, and every day it seems ethologists and other observers of animal behavior are revealing just how complex and varied are animals' lives and minds. Yet today, many of the people working to give disenfranchised human groups a voice and freedom from tyranny still refuse to acknowledge that nonhuman animals should also be free of exploitation. Regardless of which group is being victimized, is it not the same type of mental conditioning that allows us to deny the fundamental desire for life and freedom from pain to a particular group based on their color, gender, religion, sexuality, or species? I want my children to grow up understanding that animals are not things, that they deserve our respect and at the very least the freedom to live their lives unfettered and among their own.

The Horrors of Animal Abuse

At the time my husband and I started dating and for a while after we were married, I had a job as a biodecontamination specialist for a large pharmaceutical corporation. Much of my time was spent inside factory farms, lab animal–testing facilities, and pharmaceutical manufacturing plants. I would tour these places to understand the individual difficulties that each facility was having controlling the growth of microorganisms, and then help the facility to establish a program to manage the problem more successfully. What I saw there firsthand inspired me to become a vegan.

Although I was successful in my job, on some workdays I could retain my composure only long enough to come home and break down in tears at the horrors I'd seen. While consulting in a hatchery (a factory where hundreds of thousands of chicken eggs are incubated in large walk-in incubators and a certain number hatch out each day), I observed newly hatched chicks being removed from their hatching trays and placed onto a conveyer belt to get their first round of vaccinations before being packed into boxes for shipping to the growers. (Free range and organic chickens usually come from these places as well.) Large carts about six feet tall loaded with trays each holding dozens of newly hatched chicks, discarded shells, and eggs that failed to hatch were wheeled over to a window. There, three male workers unloaded the newborn chicks and tossed them through a window onto a conveyer belt.

After the live chicks were removed, the remaining contents got dumped into the trash. Then the empty cart was wheeled away to make room for the next. Were it not for my noticing a couple of really active chicks jumping over the sides of the trays and falling softly to the floor, my eyes might never have looked down. The falling chicks landed safely and proceeded to run around—stepping as they did over the half-smashed bodies of other chicks (alive and struggling to get unstuck from their own blood and guts, which glued them to the floor) who had fallen off the previous cart and then been run over by it as it was wheeled away. I wondered why nobody bothered to retrieve the fallen, unhurt chicks and return them to the cart before they too got smashed. I looked up at the men. They were leaning against the wall, puffing on their cigarettes and telling jokes, waiting for the conveyer belt to clear to make room for more chicks. It seemed as though everyone but me was oblivious to the suffering. Sad as I was for the half-smashed chicks, I later realized they were the luckiest chicks in the hatchery.

I will spare you the details of the other experiences I had. Needless to say, because of them I made the connection between what I ate and the suffering of others. I became passionate about not wanting my personal food choices to be the economic fuel that enabled practices like these to continue. Several months after adopting a vegan diet, I met my husband-to-be. I was almost thirty when my lifelong ambition of motherhood came face to face with my new-found interest in veganism.

I couldn't help but see some similarities between the behavior of the workers in the hatchery and the indifference that humans have exhibited towards other humans during our darkest times. What was it about our culture or our upbringing, I asked myself, that could allow us to ignore or rationalize the suffering of others? I thought of all the stories of people caught up by mob psychology and doing things they normally would never consider. If I was going to bring children into the world, there had to be things I could do to help them be compassionate people and make conscious choices to reduce rather then enable suffering. Veganism was a place to start.

Every year, in the United States alone, forty-one million cows, 117 million pigs, 322 million turkeys, twenty-four million ducks, five million sheep, and over eight *billion* chickens are killed for food. That means more birds and mammals die violent deaths every year in America just to make meat than there are humans currently inhabiting the entire planet. It means a staggering one million animals are killed *every hour*. How much suffering can we justify merely on the basis of appetite?

The overwhelming majority of these animals live wretched lives. Testicles, nipples, horns, tails, beaks, and toes are frequently removed without anesthesia. The animals are kept for extended periods of time in spaces so crowded and small that stretching their bodies fully and turning around are impossibilities. When I visited swine farms where pigs were confined in huge buildings, the stench of ammonia from the pig urine (even outside the building) was overpowering. Passing through the inside briefly for about two minutes made me feel as though I was suffocating. Workers generally wear respirators to protect their lungs from damage by the concentrated ammonia, yet the pigs must live continuously in this environment without respirators. The day they get to breathe fresh air is the day they are trucked to the slaughterhouse—often in open-air trucks. If the weather is bitterly cold this is not only painful, but pigs can freeze to the sides of the truck.

The Environmental Impact
The environmental impact of raising and killing animals in such numbers and so intensively is devastating. According to Howard Lyman in his book *Mad Cowboy*, million-year-old aquifers are being drained, and communities are fighting over rights to siphon off river water for their needs, just so that seventy percent of the water used in the eleven western states can be dedicated to raising animals for food. While a quarter of the world's population goes to sleep each night without sufficient food, we are feeding more and more food to animals so we can eat them. Since roughly sixteen pounds of grain are fed to a cow to make one pound of beef, the discrepancy in efficiency is glaring. An acre of prime land can produce 40,000 pounds of potatoes, 30,000 pounds of carrots, 50,000 pounds of tomatoes, or 250 pounds of beef. If you have a starving population or limited fertile land, which diet would seem the preferable one?

Mad Cowboy explains how animal agriculture uses up fossil fuels and spews out pollutants. Lyman points out that it takes the equivalent of a gallon of gasoline to produce one pound of beef, while, for the average family of four eating a meat-based diet, the amount of energy used to supply them with a year's worth of beef produces about as much pollution as the average car does in six months of use.

Unfortunately, developing countries that historically consumed plant-based diets are increasingly adopting the American diet. As well as having deleterious effects on these countries' own economies, as more and more of their precious natural resources go to meat production, this is having disastrous consequences on our quality of life here, as export of meat increases to satisfy their demand. Vast hog and poultry farms raise hundreds of thousands of animals on parcels of land too small for nature to break down the waste products before they find their way into the groundwater, lakes, and streams. Mountains and lagoons of excrement threaten drinking water, aquatic life, and air quality. In the past few years the state of North Carolina has had massive spills of sewage from giant hog-farm lagoons, which have contaminated rivers and created "dead zones," made drinking water unsafe, and forced residents many miles downwind to stay indoors with windows shut. Across the country, rural communities are fighting corporations for the right to enact zoning regulations to keep themselves from suffering North Carolina's fate.

Much of the clearing and burning of forests worldwide— which scientists believe contributes to the warming of the planet's atmosphere—is to make room for the grazing of livestock or the growing of feed grains. Removal of the trees means there is less plant matter to purify the air, which in turn creates air pollution if the trees are burned. Deforestation leads in turn to land degradation, as the soil becomes exhausted and erosion takes away precious topsoil and nutrients.

Vegan and Pregnant

I had been following a vegan diet for about two years when I became pregnant with my first child. I felt the healthiest I had ever felt and figured the way I was eating would also be good for my baby. My midwife, who considered herself mostly vegetarian, strongly encouraged healthy food choices, with an emphasis on protein for pregnant moms.

When I told her I was vegan, she grew very serious. She said that all the vegans she had helped in the past hadn't flourished during pregnancy, and she strongly suggested I add a little fish or chicken to my diet. This contradicted everything I believed in, and having worked closely with the poultry industry I knew what the birds were fed, injected with, and doused with. I could not for a moment imagine that putting their heavily poisoned bodies into mine would benefit my baby. I also knew that the fish would probably be even more loaded with toxins.

Since I had a great deal of respect for the midwife's views and experience, I examined seriously what she said. She had been through many pregnancies, and this was my first. For the first time ever, I questioned the safety of my whole-foods vegan diet. I went immediately to the medical library and researched everything I could find related to pregnancy and veganism. While there wasn't much, the few studies I did find confirmed not only that a vegan diet could be safe, but that it actually reduced the risk of a woman developing preeclampsia—one of the more common complications of pregnancy.[1]

In addition, the medical journal articles suggested another benefit—the breast milk of women on a vegan diet contained fewer sorts of environmental contaminants. As I mentioned earlier, there also was information suggesting that juvenile diabetes risk might be lower in lifelong vegans. I acquired a copy of Dr. Michael Klaper's *Pregnancy, Children and the Vegan Diet*, which was very reassuring and clearly identified the nutritional requirements for a healthy vegan pregnancy. I also contacted the Physicians Committee for Responsible Medicine (PCRM) and the Vegetarian Resource Group (VRG), and both of them sent me materials addressing vegan pregnancy. What really reassured me, however, was the book *Spiritual Midwifery* by Ina Mae Gaskin. *Spiritual Midwifery* is filled with inspiring stories of women who chose to give birth at home on The Farm, the vegan community I mentioned at the beginning of this book. At the back of *Spiritual Midwifery*, Gaskin presents the birth statistics from 1970 to 1979, during which time midwives managed over a thousand births at The Farm. The statistics are exceptional—926 of the births were delivered at The Farm. Thirty-seven of the births were considered high risk and the babies were delivered in the hospital. In all, there were two cases of preeclampsia, no maternal deaths, fifteen C-sections, and generally very good outcomes for the babies.[2]

These statistics are particularly extraordinary in light of the fact that the ages of the mothers ranged from 16 to 42, and The Farm had a reputation for taking in young unwed mothers with no means of support.

Unfortunately, there is a dearth of books offering support to mothers wanting to be vegan during pregnancy. One book I read, *Vegetarian Pregnancy* by Sharon Yntema, although pleasurable to read, actually made me more anxious about being pregnant and vegan. It seemed to have an awful lot of case histories of women who started out vegan at the beginning of pregnancy, but felt sure their body was telling them to add a few animal products. Pregnant women have enough anxieties to begin with, and vegan pregnant women probably even more because everyone around them is telling them their diet isn't safe for their baby. I turned to books like Yntema's, needing support and reassurance, and I didn't get it. In retrospect, I wonder if a woman craving meat during pregnancy is perhaps just getting a message from her body that she needs more protein. A daily soymilk smoothie might just curb those cravings if made a regular part of the diet.

Somehow, I managed to find enough data to reassure myself that I was eating healthily and I remained vegan throughout my pregnancy. When it was all over, my midwife, who by now had spent some time at our house and saw how we really ate, commented that none of the other vegans she'd known had eaten the way we did. In other words, these other vegans were not eating lots of whole foods, healthy servings of protein-rich beans, and soy products rather than junk food. Now, instead of suggesting to her vegan clients that they add some animal products to their diet, she gives them my number.

Avoiding Dairy Products

When you're a pregnant vegan, many people think you should be eating dairy products. When I was pregnant the first time, some family members expressed concern that I was not drinking any milk. They were concerned my baby would not get enough calcium or protein, and my abstinence from what they considered nature's most perfect food challenged the very foundation of their entire nutrition belief system. My attempts to soothe their anxiety were futile, since their beliefs were not based upon facts but upon an advertising campaign so pervasive many people never even realized it was just propaganda.

This is hardly surprising. Most people who grow up in the United States learn about nutrition from the dairy industry, which donates "educational materials" to schools across the country. So successful has the penetration of our consciousness been that most Americans consider it an unassailable "truth" that milk is an essential part of their diet. This is why we should be ever aware of who is dispensing information in our schools.

The fact is that cow's milk is nature's most perfect food . . . for calves. Its high protein content is designed to grow a big, bulky body fast. Human milk is much lower in protein and higher in essential fatty acids than cow's milk. Human milk is designed for rapid brain growth while plain cow's milk fed exclusively to an infant will cause death. Cow's milk and human milk are very high in the sugar lactose and, as infants, humans produce the enzyme lactase, which helps in the breakdown of this milk sugar. Around age five, many people (especially those of African, Asian, Middle Eastern, and Native American ancestry) no longer produce this enzyme and become lactose intolerant and may experience gas, bloating, and cramping whenever they consume dairy products.

This is actually a good thing—these people's bodies are giving them an early warning of the fact they shouldn't be putting dairy products into their bodies. Cow's milk also contains a number of proteins that may cause allergic reactions in people. One protein, bovine serum albumen (BSA), is thought to be a possible trigger for juvenile diabetes. Another protein, casein, is not only a cause of allergies, but generates a lot of mucus.[3]

In as short a time as a week, many people who stop eating dairy products feel much better. Because dairy fat is linked with both cancer and heart disease, many people have resorted to drinking skimmed cow's milk for their health. However, although skimmed cow's milk contains much less fat, it is more likely to elicit allergic reactions because all that's left is protein and lactose.

Every drop of cow's milk, including the organic kind, is loaded with dozens of biologically active compounds such as hormones. We don't know yet what their cumulative effect is. While some scientists argue that the hormones in cow's milk get destroyed by the acid in our stomachs and thus are rendered inactive, Robert Cohen, author of *Milk: The Deadly Poison*, points out that nature designed cow's milk as a hormone delivery system, since cows need to pass certain hormones on to their babies. Cohen says that drinking cow's milk temporarily neutralizes the stomach's acid, and the fat serves to further insulate the hormones from attack. One hormone found in cow's milk, IGF-1, is a powerful growth promoter in infants. However, beyond infancy, it is a powerful promoter of cancer. IGF-1 is found in every drop of cow's milk, and has been found in higher concentrations in milk from cows that have been treated with recombinant bovine growth hormone (rBGH), an artificial hormone that many cows in the United States have been given in order to stimulate greater production of milk.

Vegan and Pregnant—Again

When I became pregnant with my second child, I was already the mother of an active four-year-old. As I indicated earlier, I was having a tough year and my diet, although still vegan, was not as healthful as it could have been. My pregnancy had gotten off to a bad start when I indulged my taste for sweets and fat—the only things that seemed appetizing in my slightly queasy first trimester. I remember joking with friends that if the food I was eating didn't derive at least half of its calories from fat, then I wasn't interested in eating it.

To my amazement, I found I was barely gaining weight. I ate lots and lots of fruit, avocados, olives, and nuts. I wanted only things I could grab and eat; I had no motivation to cook; I was moody and constantly tired; and my joints ached. In addition, I had occasional heart palpitations. I felt eighty years old! Even though my midwife thought everything was fine, I couldn't shake the feeling that something just wasn't right. For the first time in years I didn't feel healthy!

I decided to call Dr. Michael Klaper, a doctor whose book I'd read, and whose dedication and thoroughness I'd been impressed with. Dr. Klaper counseled me to go to my family practice doctor and ask for a full examination, and gave me a list of things to specifically ask the doctor to check. Dr. Klaper also instructed me to have a complete blood count and a check of my serum B-12 levels.

Vitamin B-12 (cobalamin) is an essential vitamin produced only by bacteria living in the soil, water, or our intestines. Unfortunately it is produced in a part of our intestines downstream from where our body can absorb it. Animals eating unwashed plant matter obtain B-12 produced by bacteria clinging to the outer surfaces of these foods. They concentrate this B-12 in their tissues. This is how B-12 comes to be found in meat and dairy products. We need only a very tiny amount to prevent deficiencies—just one to four micrograms per week—and we are capable of storing B-12 for several years, so a deficiency will not occur overnight.

However, a deficiency of B-12 is serious. Because Americans live in such a hygienic environment—adding chlorine to our water, which kills B-12–producing bacteria, thoroughly washing our fruits and veggies, etc.—a modern diet based solely on plant foods is not likely to provide adequate B-12 (although primitive humans living on plant foods would not likely have had such a problem)! Serious neurological damage can occur with B-12 deficiency, so it is very important to make sure you have a reliable source of it in your diet. Sometimes symptoms are not obvious—tingling or loss of feeling in the hands and feet and memory problems. Recent studies have suggested that long-term vegans who do not consume B-12 supplements or B-12 fortified foods may have a metabolic deficiency of B-12 even though their serum B-12 levels appear satisfactory. (A more reliable test of B-12 status is a urine test that measures methylmalonic acid and is available at Norman Clinical Laboratory, 1-800-397-7408 or www.b12.com.) Early signs of deficiency can be masked by consumption of folic acid (abundant in leafy greens).

Many foods that supposedly contain B-12, such as blue-green algae, spirulina, seaweed, and tempeh, actually contain mostly B-12 analogs that do us no good and compete for absorption with real B-12. Red Star Vegetarian Support Formula Nutritional Yeast, and some fortified soymilks and rice milks or other fortified foods, *are* good sources of this vitamin. Pregnant women and children especially need to have a reliable source of B-12 in their diet. If a nursing mother's diet contains sufficient B-12, then her baby will get it from her milk. The easiest thing to do is include a sublingual B-12 supplement (methylcobalamin is best) every other day, and then you can just forget about this issue entirely!

Once these tests were completed, Dr. Klaper wanted me to call him with the results.

I went to a private laboratory and had the blood work done.[4] Unfortunately, when I then called my regular doctor for an appointment, I was unable to get our regular family practice doctor, so I scheduled with his new partner. This doctor just wouldn't take my concerns seriously. Although my blood pressure was normal and I had no swelling, I had to keep asking him to do the things that Dr. Klaper had said, like palpate my lymph glands. It was a struggle the whole way.

After Dr. Klaper had a chance to go over all my results, he suggested that I take a prenatal supplement (which I had not been doing), try to eat eighty grams of protein a day, and take a daily dose of vitamin B-12 spray. He felt that I was borderline low on protein, B-12, and iron. By this time I was about six months into my pregnancy. I started keeping diet sheets, and was shocked to realize that I was not getting as much protein as I thought. Too much of my diet was in fact fruit, salads, and fats like avocado.

I started making sure I had a good serving of beans each day, plus I had a protein shake made with soy milk, tofu, and protein powder. Gradually energy picked up and during my last trimester I felt in the best health of my whole pregnancy.

Although my baby was almost nine pounds at birth and we both ended up fine, my baby's smaller-than-normal placenta made us all wonder if my feeling so lousy was due to not getting adequate protein. Thankfully, I followed my intuition. I believe Dr. Klaper's advice was right-on. Although I've heard many times it's easy to get enough protein on a vegan diet—as long as you consume enough calories— I now believe that pregnancy is a whole different matter with respect to protein needs. I think the daily servings of beans and soy products made a huge difference.

The vitamin B-12 supplement may have also been critical. Although, as I have said, we can store several years' worth of B-12, these stores are generally not available to a fetus. A woman must have a regular source of B-12 in her diet for the baby to draw from.

While I make sure to include B-12–fortified foods in my diet, these may not have been sufficient to meet the demands of pregnancy. According to Dr. Klaper, if vitamin B-12 is taken in pill form it often is not well-absorbed since it needs to bind to a factor present in saliva for absorption. Using a B-12 spray, or lozenge and allowing it to sit under the tongue, is generally much more effective.

My experience illustrates that a vegan diet before, during, and after pregnancy is not harmful to yourself or the child. In fact, it may well be the opposite: A well-planned vegan diet reduces the risk of preeclampsia and diabetes, and decreases the amount of pesticide in the mother's milk. It is a compassionate way to start a new life.

Raising Vegan Children

The real challenges of raising children vegan actually started after they began eating solid food. At that point we had to deal with others who didn't necessarily share our diet offering food to our children as well. Because our culture revolves around food, we have had to find creative ways to balance our own ideals with the social expectations of non-vegan family and friends.

On those occasions when we find ourselves present at a family event that takes place at a non-vegan restaurant, we've learned a few coping skills. We always have our daughter sit directly in between my husband and me (the result of an occasion when one relative nearly fed our daughter non-vegan food as she sat on his lap). We secretly pack some little trinkets and games and smuggle them into the restaurant. Then, when dinner is over we introduce the goodies one at a time to keep her happily in her seat until all the dishes are cleared from the table. Then she is free to go sit on anyone's lap. This, we find, works very well.

Fortunately, for the most part our family honors our wishes. The only glitches have involved occasional foods that have hidden animal ingredients or ingredients that, although not derived from animals, we consider unhealthy for children. These include natural flavors, sodium caseinate, artificial colors, artificial sweeteners, and hydrogenated fats. When our daughter goes visiting, we usually send a cooler of food for her to snack from and there are no problems.

When we sent our daughter to preschool, we found out that state laws required her to eat the school's food. I explained to her teacher that, for religious reasons, we followed a special diet, and the school allowed us to send special food for our daughter. Although there is a solid basis for eating kosher food in my Jewish tradition (which I honor), the religious tradition itself is immaterial, since I believe in a compassionate creator who wants us to learn unconditional love and show respect for all of creation. Many Jewish and Christian scholars believe that the original reason for our dietary laws was as a concession to human appetite for flesh—a result of our failure to abide by God's original law, which was vegetarian. Having extensive rules about the consumption of flesh foods made eating meat inconvenient and rare. In addition, many other spiritual traditions make statements that discourage eating animals, while all major religions teach us to take care of our bodies.

North American Vegetarian Society

Not only does our religion and larger family support us in our choice, but we also make sure to reinforce our lifestyle (and have a wonderful family vacation at the same time) by visiting the North American Vegetarian Society's (NAVS) Summerfest. The Summerfest is usually held at a college campus and is the most life-affirming, intellectually stimulating, rejuvenating, and fun thing we do all year. It is also something that we can do together as a family, too. Summerfest is like summer camp, a cruise (endless all-you-can-eat vegan buffets served three times a day and prepared under the direction of Culinary Olympic medal–winning chefs), and favorite college electives all rolled into one. There is a children's center, staffed by a combination of volunteers and parents who provide structured activities. Throughout the day, there is a cornucopia of lectures, panel discussions, cooking demonstrations, and exercise classes. Topics discussed cover an incredible range of issues related to diet, health, animal rights, and the environment—there's even an exhibit area with vendors. What I find most exciting of all, however, is the caliber of speakers who mingle freely with the attendees. Because of this, I've had opportunities to talk one-on-one with some of the brightest and most inspiring people alive today.

It's not often that you can talk with the leading researchers in the fields of health and nutrition, or watch the top cookbook writers prepare their specialties, or have your thinking stretched by the greatest minds of such a rapidly growing progressive movement. I truly believe that many of the Summerfest speakers will be the visionary leaders of tomorrow. I would heartily recommend those families who are thinking of becoming vegetarians to attend the Summerfest and surround themselves with supportive friends, family, and community. You will find your feelings reinforced, encouragement for moments when you wonder whether your choices are too hard, and a marvelously nurturing environment for your children and yourself.

Dealing with Non-Vegan Partners

Your life partner can also be a source of reinforcement. Every day, I feel grateful not only that I came to veganism prior to meeting my husband, but that he agreed to raising our children this way. However, I have many friends who came to veganism or vegetarianism only *after* embarking on family life, and they have faced many challenges. While it is perhaps easier to begin raising vegan children together, you must be careful how you approach your spouse if you embarked upon family life with the implied agreement that the family would be omnivorous. It is important to build consensus rather than initiate power struggles or rebellion.

In one family I know, it was the father who gradually started moving towards a plant-based diet after years of omnivorousness. His wife and four school-aged children were all still very attached to the standard American diet, and for several years the father hoped that by merely setting the example, rather than preaching, his family would start to follow. However, year after year he failed to see any changes.

As the father continued to educate himself about the impact our dietary choices have, he became more concerned about the long-term consequences of what his family was eating. So he shifted gears slightly and started sharing little bits of information about diet and animal suffering. He provided opportunities for the children to meet people passionate about vegetarianism and let his children hear about the benefits of plant-based diets from others. Although he shared an occasional video on the topic, he continued to honor his children's food choices. He now tells me that everyone in his family has made major changes—of their own free will—such as choosing rice milk instead of cow's milk, and cutting back on or even eliminating meat-eating. With each child the process has been different. Both parents are hoping that all their children will become vegan.

In another family I know, it is the mother who shifted to a plant-based diet after marriage and children. Her husband is not enthusiastic about the changes. Their children are young. At first the mother was emphatic about wanting to protect her children from risks associated with eating animal products, but her task was daunting. Her husband, an otherwise compassionate man, was fully enmeshed in the mainstream world of work and very attached to his way of eating. As I've said before, "The deed shapes the heart," and I believe that, for many meat-eaters, eating flesh keeps the heart from fully opening up to our complicity in animals' suffering. While the mother does her best to provide her family with a variety of healthful vegetarian meals, the children are exposed to two different examples and have opportunities to consume foods the mother would prefer they didn't. Therefore, while the children are certainly being raised more healthily then the average American, they're also being exposed to more hormones, cholesterol, bad fats, animal protein, and endocrine disrupters than they would be on a whole-foods, vegan diet. They are also developing a taste for foods they may someday struggle to overcome.

Suzanne Havala, primary author of two past American Dietary Association position papers on vegetarianism and author of the *Complete Idiot's Guide to Vegetarianism*, was the product of a home where her mother was vegetarian and her father not. Her mother set the vegetarian example but never once explained why, since the father was vehemently opposed to his children being vegetarian and she wanted to keep the peace. Although the mother didn't attempt to influence anyone, eventually each of the four children began following the mother's example. Now as adults, all four children and even Suzanne's father (!) are vegetarians. Suzanne believes the fact her mother never pushed made it easy for them to follow her lead.

Victoria Moran, author of *How to Lead a Charmed Life*, describes yet another benefit of raising vegan children. Her daughter, vegan since birth, has learned to not just mindlessly go along with peers and put things into her body; instead, she makes conscious choices. This habit has paid off; now her daughter is a teenager and is able to counter pressure from her peers concerning drugs.

Before making a commitment to a partner, I strongly encourage you to consider carefully how important it is to you to have your children raised vegan (or whatever issues you and your partner disagree on). Ask whether your partner is supportive of your choice, and, if you're beyond this point, then what compromise or position would be in the best interests of your whole family. Turning a lifestyle choice into a polarizing family issue is certainly not in anyone's best interest. Quietly setting the example, and discreetly arranging for your loved ones to get information from sources not appearing to come from you, may be your best bet.

Making conscious choices about what foods you feed your family can have far-reaching impacts. It can set the stage for disease or health and can form the foundation of an ethical system that will guide and shape their lives. It can fortify them against peer pressure, and is the one thing we can all do every day to make the world safer, healthier, and more compassionate. Three times a day the deed shapes the heart. That's why I raise my children vegan.

---

1. *Southern Medical Journal*, June 1987.

2. More information on the diet of pregnant women at The Farm can also be found at the back of the *New Farm Vegetarian Cookbook*. Given The Farm's stunning outcomes of pregnant vegans birthing at home, I consider their dietary recommendations fairly credible.

3. Dairy derivatives are in everything from candy and baked goods, to crackers, some cereals, and pastas, and even soy cheese. Read labels carefully—casein, sodium caseinate, whey, and non-fat milk powder are just a few of milk's aliases.

4. I had the work done under an alias. I didn't want my private medical records to be part of some national database shared freely among certain corporations. We carry only a major medical policy to cover something that might create financial hardship for us. Other than that we pay cash at the time of services and can often negotiate discounts. We have a healthy lifestyle, and seldom have any reason to see a doctor. This saves us money. We assume full responsibility for our health care decisions and don't have to deal with any HMO or other agency trying to dictate the practitioners or services we can use.

Chapter Six
Nonviolent Discipline

ALL THE YEARS I WAS GROWING UP, I GAVE A GREAT deal of thought to how I would someday discipline my children. (Remember my aunt and her two well-behaved children?) I studied closely the families I knew to see how parents handled their children's misbehavior. I tried to find connections between the parents' approach and how well-adjusted the children were.

My own parents' discipline of me had been inconsistent, and (in comparison with my two well-behaved cousins, whom I wrote about in the first chapter) I consider myself to have been poorly behaved and obnoxious as a child. I didn't simply question authority, I challenged it continuously, and didn't know how to get along with my peers. This crippled me socially and had been a source of tremendous loneliness and sadness. I didn't want my children to grow up like me, feeling as if people didn't want to be around them.

However, those very characteristics of challenging authority and asking questions that made me so miserable as a child have served me well as an adult—now I've learned how to channel these behaviors better. I credit my parents' approach with enabling me to develop into a strong and capable free thinker who is not afraid to swim against the tide. This aspect of myself I *do* want to pass along to my children. I want them to question authority if they have reason to—but not just arbitrarily.

Initially my assessment of what helped children to be well-disciplined focused upon superficial factors. For instance, like my aunt, I believed that spanking, if administered quickly at the first sign of disobedience, was the key to good discipline. As a teenager I continued to examine the discipline of children carefully. I regularly baby-sat for dozens of families, was a camp counselor every summer for five years, and taught outdoor education. I volunteered to work one-on-one with learning disabled children and then was a nanny for a family who traveled frequently. I started my own business bringing live animals to schools and using them to conduct educational programs—something that took me into hundreds of classrooms where I scrutinized the ways teachers maintained order. In my first year of college I worked in a Montessori preschool.

Through all these experiences I was making mental notes about what worked and what didn't. Some children were delightful, some were terrors, and some parents were too preoccupied to follow through on discipline and dealt with misbehavior only when it became too disruptive, dangerous, or inconvenient to ignore. Many children, it seemed to me, lacked loving, consistent discipline. They were miserable and made sure that everyone around them was too.

My Two-Point Plan

I became convinced that there were really only two steps to raise happy, well-adjusted children. I'd watched many distraught parents ineffectively dealing with their little tyrants over the years and it was obvious their problems boiled down to the fact that they were either poorly educated about raising children or lazy. I had it all worked out in my head! When I became a parent, I decided, I would, first, amass a wealth of information about children's needs and techniques for disciplining them (the "how to" part), then, second, follow through on what I knew, all the time and no matter what. It would be easy! Boy, was I naive.

After college, I went through a training program to become a CASA (Court Appointed Special Advocate) volunteer. CASA volunteers are advocates for any child who may find him- or herself in the court system as a result of abuse, divorce, or neglect. The training program was excellent and quite comprehensive, although it was so long ago that I really only remember one thing. As a result of the compelling case that the CASA trainers made, I decided I would never hit my children. I came to see all hitting as damaging and as modeling exactly the behavior I didn't want my child to exhibit—that might makes right. I learned, and came to believe, that hitting condones violence, and that good discipline can be very effectively accomplished without ever being violent. While I continued to study families, only those families whose children were well-disciplined without using violence served as my role models. Yet, I clung to the idea that my two-point parenting program was all I would need.

There was a third part to the equation that I'd somehow failed to recognize. I don't know if no one had ever explained this to me or I just was not yet at a point where this third aspect could penetrate my consciousness.

Disciplining as a First-Time Parent

My first two years as a mother went relatively smoothly. While there were definitely challenging moments, in general I felt extremely competent as a mother and that my study of parenting had paid off. I'd even added a few new techniques along the way. Overall, I was very pleased with my two-year-old's development and behavior. I had braced myself for the "terrible twos" and they had never come. In fact from the age of eighteen months to three years, my first child hadn't cried much, and when she did it didn't last long. She'd never thrown a tantrum or tried to manipulate the situation by acting out.

This behavior I attribute to a particularly wise book called *The Aware Baby,* by Aletha Solter. In it, the author emphasizes how important it is for babies and young children to cry, since it serves as an emotional release for them—especially if they are not yet able to express their difficulties verbally—and acts as a way to deal with the endless frustration caused by being such small people in a big, confusing world. However, says Solter, the key to making crying a positive thing is to hold your baby or child while he is crying and look lovingly into his eyes without distracting him. This means no patting on the back, no bouncing, no saying, "Shhhhh." You only have to be there with him, calm and loving, she emphasizes. Every now and then, you very calmly say something like, "It's all right to cry. I know you're upset. I love you and I'll just hold you until you're done."

Solter also clearly points out that before you hold the child, you need to figure out why your baby is crying. If you can definitively rule out hunger, thirst, other physical discomforts—sleepiness, illness, etc.—then and *only then* do you sit down with your baby and help her "discharge" in this way. (I would also add that you need to consider whether this technique fits your child's own unique personality, since I do not know whether this technique may be harmful for some children.)

I remember a few times when my older daughter was a toddler and was furious about not being able to do something she wanted. It was then I put Solter's advice into practice. My daughter would struggle intensely against my holding her; she'd fight to get out of my arms—kicking, screaming, and crying. Usually, I continued to hold her firmly until she'd calmed down and would then witness a remarkable transformation. But a few times I did let her go in the midst of the upset, wondering if my restraining her was simply increasing her frustration. The minute she discovered she was free, she immediately threw herself against me or tried to climb back into my lap. It was clear she didn't really want to get away from me, but was just very upset. I definitely credit this technique with making my daughter's twos not terrible but terrific.

My younger daughter is now a toddler. She came into this world with a very passionate temperament. I haven't used this approach as much with her due to the fact that I now have two children to care

for and simply don't always have the luxury of sitting down unin-
terrupted with a screaming child for thirty or forty minutes.
However, the few times I *have* managed to create the space for us to
do this, the results have clearly indicated that this is absolutely what
she needed.

Recently we had a day when frustration after frustration had
brought my younger child to tears. Her older sister was grabbing
toys away from her, she kept falling and bumping herself while
playing, and I had thwarted her attempts to remove dirt from my
potted plants. For Sammi it was one bad thing after another.
Finally, after my husband came home, I took her and we went into
the bedroom alone. I held her on my lap and looked lovingly into
her eyes. "You've had a hard day," I said. "I think you just need a
good cry."

"No, no, no," she said, shaking her head for emphasis. She began
squirming in my lap and tried to get down, but I held her firmly and
she started crying. Within five minutes, she was letting out blood-
curdling yells. I kept my attention fully on her and made eye contact
whenever her eyes were open and smiled at her. Every time I told her
I loved her, that she could let all those sad and angry feelings out and
I would still always love her, the volume of her screams lessened a
bit. I held her firmly as she kicked, twisted, and even tried to bite me
a few times.[1] A few times when I loosened my grip to see what she
would do, she'd either slide out of my lap and then stop crying and
rest her head on my legs, or climb up and put her head on my shoulder and stop crying while sucking on her fingers.

When I said to her very softly, "I really think you need to cry
some more. Take your fingers out of your mouth so you can cry," she
did, slowly and reluctantly, and the tears would start up all over
again. A couple of times during all of this she stretched her neck up
and kissed me on the cheek. I held her until she calmed down on
her own. Her body movements went from jerky and forceful to gentle flexing motions with her fingers and toes. After it was all over, she
was much more relaxed. She played much more happily with her

sister, and when I entered the room she spontaneously came over to me and gave me hugs and kisses and then went back to her play.

Solter suggests in her book that not having adequate opportunities to "discharge" negative emotions like this can be a source of mental and physical ill health. I have found that after a good discharge my babies are eager to cooperate—which, after all, is the goal of good discipline.

Things Turn Difficult

During my third year of parenting (before my second child had been conceived), my life took a dramatic turn. My husband and I were faced with a difficult situation that required us to choose between standing up for a principle or doing what we thought would be best for our family. The experience changed me profoundly and left me feeling very disillusioned with our American culture. Even though I fully realized I still had a life filled with enormous blessings, my awareness of this became cerebral rather than emotional. I fell into a mild depression.

As I found out very rapidly, it was one thing to attempt to carry out steps one and two of my parenting plan when my life was basically stress free; it was entirely another to try to do it having just come through a life-changing trauma and feeling totally demoralized. I was often angry, and found myself very intolerant of my daughter's normal three-year-old behavior. We moved to a new home and I got pregnant. I kept hoping to put it all behind me and get on with life, but my state deteriorated even more.

That's when I came to realize that knowing how to parent and consistently following through were simply not enough. My plan to raise happy, well-disciplined children depended upon a third thing: dealing with my own emotional condition. I realized that it is often not what we do, but the emotions *behind* our action, that makes the most impact on our children.

Now I understand why it can be so challenging for parents to be consistent with discipline or exhibit respect and compassion all the time. Feelings of stress, depression, disappointment, loss, or simply being out of sorts can hamper our ability to parent the way we'd like and increase the probability we will go on autopilot and treat our children the way our parents treated us as children when they were stressed. While I have never hit my children, I have unfortunately come to realize that my words and attitude can be just as damaging. The upside of this realization, however, is that I'm developing more compassion for my own parents. On a very deep level, I now realize that all of us parents are working to improve upon the parenting we received. We all do the best we can.

The Key Third Component of Parenting

So now my plan for raising well-adjusted and disciplined children has a third part, which I think of as working to develop my own maturity and become conscious about the dynamics that shape my own moods and behavior. For this, I have found that studying the Bowen Family Systems Theory is very helpful. Bowen is a theory and approach to mental health that incorporates many of the discoveries of biology and anthropology. At its core, Bowen proposes (like poet John Donne) that no one is an island and that the degree of functioning and mental health we experience in our lives is related to the family system we're part of. By working to build solid and calm connections with members of our extended family, we provide the best possible chance our children will be well-adjusted.

I have found that the best way to be peaceful and less reactive with my own children is to work on my staying connected and calm with my own parents, sisters, and other relatives. I believe this is the best insurance for the mental health of my family's future generations. (I talk more about Bowen Family Systems Theory in Chapter Nine.)

One of my all-time favorite writers whose perspective is very consistent with Bowen is the British social anthropologist Sheila

Kitzinger. Kitzinger has written extensively about women's lives and is an authority on cross-cultural studies of motherhood, pregnancy, birth, and midwifery. One of the things Kitzinger points out is that in some ways middle-class women in Western cultures have a greater challenge in mothering than women of peasant societies. When mothers look around in peasant societies, they see all the other women mothering in pretty much the same way. But, in the West, says Kitzinger, we have many "experts" saying contradictory things and giving many options about how to mother. This causes us to constantly compare our mothering, wondering if we are "good enough" mothers and giving our children every advantage we can. Kitzinger emphasizes there is no one "right" way to mother and that mothering is a very complex and unique expression of a mother's own personality in the context of her particular culture interacting with the personalities of each of her children. I find Kitzinger's work to be very calming and beneficial to my mothering.

One Mormon couple I know with four wonderful children have told me that their philosophy is to try to parent their children in the same way they believe the creator tries to teach humankind—through natural consequences. For them, this approach to discipline has been an evolution. They started out much more authoritarian, but now feel that the creator doesn't punish us for misbehavior but simply allows us to experience the natural consequences of our actions. This, they feel, is an appropriate model for us to follow when guiding our children. To me, this is a wise and compassionate approach.

The Discipline Theories of John Rosemond

I have also found tremendous value in the ideas of child psychologist and author John Rosemond. His old-fashioned, no-nonsense approach provides a good fit for my controlling personality. He strongly encourages parents to take charge, as this is critical for a child's feelings of security. When a child knows clearly that his parents are in control it allows him to believe his parents are powerful enough to protect him and keep him safe. It's one thing for a parent to occasionally ask her child where she'd like to eat tonight, but another when a child's whining or insistence influences many family decisions—this is very unsettling for the child. Children like these become more and more demanding, trying to find firm boundaries where they can feel their parents have sufficient power to protect them.

John Rosemond's work helps me feel comfortable about "taking charge." He points out that we don't always have to have a good reason for why we make certain decisions—that every day there are numerous decisions that must be made for the family to function and someone must make these decisions. Many decisions, he notes, are simply arbitrary—for instance, which route to take to get somewhere—but they still must be made, and, in most cases, it's simplest for the parent to make them.

Parenting is such a guilt-ridden endeavor (especially for mothers) that reading Rosemond's work helps me lighten up on myself. Rosemond is also good for those times when I'm simply out of patience, out of steam, and simply need my children to go play by themselves and leave me alone. According to Rosemond, mothers should give themselves license to tell their children to leave them alone much more often.

I must temper these words of praise for Rosemond's work, however, with this warning. On the surface his approach is very attractive. It promises to put parents fully in control, alleviate any guilt they may feel over their decisions, and allow them to be smugly numb to any self-doubts about what they're doing. I do, however, think that sometimes he goes too far: He can be extremely punitive; he talks about sending children to their rooms for the entire day for offenses that are neither life-threatening nor immoral; he approves of spanking. While some of his ideas are extremely helpful, work wonderfully, and provide a very good balance to some of those cultural norms that often disempower parents, in my heart I know that to rely too much on his philosophy would violate my own life's principles, compromise the degree of connection I have with my children, and dull the spark and love of life I see in them—even though it would no doubt give me very well-behaved children and much more free time for myself. I want more for my children and more connection with them than exclusively relying on Rosemond's philosophy would provide.

In one of his books, Rosemond rails against what he calls "democratic parenting," which he believes is very misguided. When I read this, I felt certain that in his tirade against democratic parenting he was referring to another of my other favorite parenting authors: Rudolf Dreikurs, author of *Children the Challenge*. Although some of Dreikurs' language is dated (his book came out in the early 1960s), the essence of what he says remains quite relevant. Although Rosemond may disagree, I see many similarities between Rosemond and Dreikurs. Both emphasize the importance of children being contributing members of the family; both suggest that a child who wields too much power in the family feels insecure because he doesn't really feel like his parents are in control and, therefore, capable of keeping him safe. Such a child makes himself and everyone else miserable as he continuously presses the limits. However, the two authors differ in their suggestions of how to accomplish this. While Rosemond, as I've said, is very authoritarian, Dreikurs believes that, as our culture has evolved from autocracy to democracy, so authoritarianism has become less effective with children. Dreikurs says that children recognize we live in a democracy and expect to live by democratic rules and natural consequences (sometimes orchestrated by parents) to shape their behavior.

A fourth author from my list of most-loved books on discipline is Barbara Coloroso, author of *Kids Are Worth It! Giving Your Child the Gift of Inner Discipline*. Coloroso takes much of Dreikurs' philosophy and packages it in a much more readable form, with examples relevant to how we live today. Her book epitomizes what nonviolent discipline is all about. She advocates allowing your children to make most of their

own decisions as long as they are not life-threatening, morally problematic, or unhealthful. While I agree wholeheartedly with Coloroso's
approach, I personally find it difficult to implement much of the time.
I simply haven't learned to give up that much control.

Mixing and Matching Parenting Tips

As Sheila Kitzinger points out, how we "mother" or "father" is a
unique expression of who we are. Each of us must find the best mix
of all that we are exposed to, consistent with our fundamental values
and within our capabilities, given our own life struggles. You can pick
and choose elements from seemingly inconsistent philosophies if you
pay attention to whether the particular approach seems to help you
feel either more or less connected to your child. Sometimes it is only
in retrospect that I realize something I did, although perhaps useful
for solving a particular problem, just didn't feel right to me. For
instance, during a particularly stressful time, my older daughter (then
five years old) started attempting to monopolize my attention by asking me questions unrelentingly. One after the other the questions
kept coming—most of them to which she hardly gave any thought at
all in asking them. All other family conversations took backstage to
her endless barrage, and I found myself barely able to think if we
were in the same room together. My attempts to help her see that she
needed to give other people a chance to initiate conversation and to
pay attention to the situation before questioning weren't getting
through. I was nearly at wit's end.

Finally, in desperation I resorted to a Rosemond-type solution. I
made up three sets of coupons and placed them in a prominent
place. She was allotted twenty red coupons for general questions
about things, eight blue coupons for questions asking me to help her
with something, and five green coupons to ask me to come look at
something. I explained to her that each day we would play a game
(something she initially thought was great). We'd start out with the
full set of coupons, I told her, and every time she asked a question
one of these would get used up. If she still had one left of each color

an hour before her normal bedtime, she'd be allowed to stay up until her normal time. But if she didn't, then she'd go to bed an hour earlier (giving me somewhat of a break).

Going into this little exercise I fully expected that it would probably take a month or so to "retrain" her. However, on the first day she "got it" and by the third day things were still going very well. But something didn't feel right. I had second thoughts about stifling her questions simply because I couldn't cope. I, therefore, told her that she had done such a good job with our "game" that as long as she could continue being more respectful with her questions we wouldn't do this anymore. She was relieved to know she wouldn't have to worry about the possibility of going to bed early. We've had no more problems with her asking too many questions.

Some problems have been resolved without my ever feeling any regrets about our approach. Before our second child could walk, we never put shoes on her feet—she didn't like them and we felt going barefoot was better for her developing feet. However, once she learned to walk, we wanted her to have shoes on any time she was outside, to protect her from thorns and rocks. Unfortunately, she was adamant about not wearing shoes. When I put them on her, she sat on the floor and screamed while trying to take them off her feet. It seemed cruel to force her to wear them, so we tried a different approach. We told her that only children with shoes on were allowed to get down on the ground outside. She still refused to put them on. Each time we planned to go outside we would ask her, "Would you like to put on shoes so you can play outside?" The first few times, she made it clear she was not about to wear shoes. We were very nonchalant as we went on with our plans but said nothing else about her shoes. We either left her indoors while one of us stayed behind, or we took her with us—but confined her to the backpack and wouldn't allow her to get out of it to play with her sister. After several days of this, she had a complete change of attitude about shoes. As I had done several previous times, I told her we were getting ready to go outside, and then added, "Any children with shoes on can go out." This time she went and got her shoes, handed them to me, and sat down on the floor and waited for me to put them on her feet. That day she learned to walk with shoes on her feet and since that time we've had no problems putting shoes on her.

Releasing the Need to Be Perfect

Fortunately, children are pretty resilient. We don't have to be perfect. I think it's good for our children to see us working to parent the best we can in a way consistent with our own values, and to sometimes see us making mistakes. I admit to them when I think I've made a mistake but don't dwell on it: I simply apologize and then move on. As my examples illustrate, I've found it useful to use elements of both authoritarianism and natural consequences. While it comes much more naturally to me to be authoritarian, I do believe natural consequences will better prepare my children for life on their own. Of course, I utilize both of these approaches upon a firm foundation of attachment-style parenting. This offers my children the best chance to become thinking, compassionate people who will impact the world positively.

More on Attachment-Style Parenting

Attachment-style parenting, as I mentioned in Chapter One, is the focus of the work of William Sears M.D. and Martha Sears. The Searses describe how good discipline must be built upon a foundation of really knowing and understanding your child. Every time I find myself starting to feel as if my relationship with my children is heading in an adversarial direction, I reread a section of their book *The Discipline Book*. It helps me to step back, regroup, and usually discover a way of meeting both their needs and mine in a way that brings us closer together and calmer. The Searses point out how children can obey out of either fear or respect. One problem with discipline based upon fear is that when you turn your back it is more likely to fall apart. When your children obey because they have a deep respect for you rather than fear of the consequences, they are less likely to stray again when you're not there.

After years of observations, reading, and my own experience, I realize there is no one right way. Every child is unique and each family different in terms of the dynamics. Some families who have chosen lifestyles very different from my own seem to have happy, well-adjusted children capable of interacting with a wide range of people. There appears to be much love and respect among the parents and the children. Ultimately, we must each find our own way.

We began laying the foundation for discipline in our home when our children were born. It started, as the Searses suggested, by tuning into our babies and working to understand and meet their needs. By responding promptly and compassionately to their cries, we earned their trust. Once our children could understand us sufficiently, we started to set limits that communicated to them that they were *part* of our family and not the *center* of it. This started in the latter half of the first year. For instance, I would say to my six-month-old, who was crying and wanting to nurse, "I'll nurse you in just a minute after I finish up what I am doing." Initially, these delays would not exceed five minutes. But, gradually, depending upon the situation (I wouldn't delay a hungry baby more than this, but I might make a bored and mobile baby wait a little longer while I did something else), our babies have learned that in a family everyone's needs must be balanced.

Because babies have enough frustrating things to deal with just mastering their own bodies and trying to make sense of the world, it is important to structure your home as much as possible so that it doesn't add to their frustration. Once a baby is mobile, she or he needs safe places to explore. Put the things you don't want them to touch out of reach; minimize your battles. Make it easy for your baby to see herself cooperating with your family's routines—this will set the tone for future interactions. There'll be plenty of opportunities to teach her what "no" means when you are out and about. We have never used a playpen since these tend to deprive a baby of the very types of exploration, movement, and experiences our biology craves and our evolution programmed us to need in order to maximize neurological development.

By about eighteen months of age a toddler is ready to learn about "time-outs." With our firstborn, we set a little chair in the corner and put her in it for one or two minutes for offenses like touching the buttons on the oven. We would firmly tell her, "That's not for babies. You're in time-out." We were amazed that she never once tried to get out of the chair, until we came back and said, "All right, you may get up now." With our second child, we weren't sure if this would work with her; we imagined her just simply getting up and walking away. If this *had* happened, I would have sat with her and held her in the chair. Instead, however, we decided to put a really tall chair—a counter chair—in the time-out spot. She has never tried to get out of this chair, since it's too far off the ground. In this way, our younger child has always remained in the time-out chair until we allow her to move.

One thing that really helps with discipline is to always expect your children to do as you say. We no longer use chair time-outs for our older daughter; now we send her to her bedroom. Despite being filled with fun things, this acts as a deterrent because it removes her from the hub of social activity—where she most wants to be. Sometimes I give her verbal directions to go there; at other times I simply pick her up without saying a word and deposit her in there with instructions not to come out. A few times, when she was very enraged about something and happened to be going through a more obstinate period, she would scream "No!" at me after I set her in her room and turned to walk out. I'd hear her charge after me but I would never respond to her challenge and I never looked back—I just kept on walking. By not looking back to see if she was obeying me, I communicated to her that I fully expected her to do as I said.

I also averted many power struggles. I knew that if I looked back, she would have thought that I didn't expect her to obey.

Most of the time this tactic was sufficient for her to realize she had better go back into her room. However, once she did follow me out of her room and all the way into the kitchen and I was forced to address her transgression. I looked at her very sternly, deliberately shook my head, and then slowly and expressing grave disappointment told her that she would now have to stay in her room much longer. She went right back in.

Never Argue with Your Children

I cannot emphasize enough how important it is never to argue with your child. To do so plainly conveys that you are not in control. There is no rule that says you must answer every question or respond to every challenge. If you have given instructions or an answer to something and it is not negotiable, do not get drawn into further discussion or defense of your position. Sometimes silence is the strongest response you have! The same goes for threatening. If my children are leaning back in the counter chairs, I simply tell them that it is not safe and that if they do it again they'll have to get down. The next time they do it, I simply walk over and remove them from the chairs without saying a word.

My husband and I both feel strongly that our children should have many opportunities to contribute to family life. Not only does this take some of the load off us, but it really helps the children feel good about themselves. It gives them an important sense of what their place is in our family community. When my children start to become more demanding and less cooperative, it is a sign to me that they need *more* responsibility. Our toddler doesn't yet have assigned chores, but when she spills something we ask her to go get the floor towel, and she is able to wipe up most of the spill herself. We frequently ask her to help us or get things for us and she is eager to do so.

Our five-year-old does have set chores. Every morning she is expected to clean her room and water a portion of our houseplants. At first, we found ourselves having to remind her to do this every day. So we established a new rule: Her room must be clean before she comes out of it in the morning and the houseplants must be watered before she can have breakfast. Now both things happen every morning—usually without any input from us. She is also required to set the table each night for dinner. If she fails to do this on her own, I do it—without saying a word—and then inform her that she will have to wash the dishes after dinner instead. In addition to these daily chores, she knows she is expected to pitch in and help with various projects around the house that may come up: cleaning floors, picking up toys, fetching things, etc. These she usually does cheerfully—if she sees the rest of us doing these same things too.

Sibling Competition versus Sibling Rivalry

The biggest challenge we face these days with respect to discipline involves the behavior of our two children with each other. John Rosemond says that sibling *competition* is normal and nothing to worry about. It only becomes sibling *rivalry* when an adult gets involved. While it is extremely hard to stand by and watch our five-year-old rip a toy out of the hands of our toddler, we've found that getting involved in these disputes is totally ineffective and only increases the frequency with which they occur. Our misguided intervention reinforces for our children their perception that one of them is a victim and the other a victimizer. When our toddler was younger, we intervened constantly to protect her from abuse (which we feel was appropriate before she was mobile and semi-verbal), but we soon noticed that she was screaming in anticipation that her older sister might do something. It was obvious that what we were doing was not helping the two of them to get along.

Fortunately we got a hold of a very enlightened book, *Siblings without Rivalry: How to Help Your Children Live Together So You Can*

Too, by Adele Faber and Elaine Mazlish. Although the book could have made its wonderful points with many fewer words, it was worth plodding through to get to the gems. We found the authors' suggestions extremely helpful. Now when there is a dispute we generally stay out of it. If, after a couple of minutes, the children haven't worked things out or the intensity builds up too much, then I intervene in such a way as not to take sides. If the dispute is over a toy (which is usually the case), I take it away and matter-of-factly tell them that since they can't figure out how to play together with it nicely, then no one will get to play with it.

Occasionally things get so heated that my toddler's coping skills get overwhelmed, in which case I will pick her up and offer to hold her until she feels ready to go back and play. If there have been several escalations in the space of a morning (very unusual these days), then I restrict the two of them to separate parts of the house and forbid them to play together for a while. The results of this approach have been phenomenal: My children are getting better and better at playing together, having more fun with each other, and needing assistance from me much less. Our children are learning to resolve their own problems without needing us to intervene.

The Essential Part: Love and Affection

There is one last part I feel is critical to good discipline: love and affection. I aim to balance out every reprimand, criticism, or insistence that I'm busy with at least five loving gestures. I am constantly telling my children that I love them, giving them unsolicited hugs and kisses, pointing out the things they do that I appreciate, and letting them know I am thankful every day that they came into my life. After all—that's why I had children!

---

1. Normally I would sternly tell her, "No, we don't bite." But when I am helping her discharge like this, I don't say a thing—I'm just careful to keep my hands away from her mouth. This is not the time to teach her self-control but instead to make it safe for her to be out of control and feel safe letting go of some possibly frighteningly intense feelings.

Chapter Seven
Creating a Peaceful Home

STRUCTURE DETERMINES FUNCTION. ENGINEERS, architects, chiropractors, and physiologists all know this to be true. Enlightened parents know this as well. Once you determine the values, ideals, and ethics most important to you, you are ready to make conscious choices about how you will structure your home to facilitate the sharing of your values with your children.

The material items we bring into our home and the rules we have guiding the behavior of people in our home are all expressions of who we are, what we value, and what path we wish our family to travel. While it may at first seem overly controlling to have clearly defined house rules, any family has rules, although they may not have conceptualized them as such. Do you allow people to smoke in your house? Are visitors allowed to leapfrog from one piece of furniture to another? How would you feel about someone bringing pornography or racist materials into your home? What about frying up a steak in your kitchen?

While it is commendable to work towards "tolerating" other people's life choices, we also need to set an example for our children of sometimes taking a stand that may be socially risky but consistent with our own ethics. We cannot stop other people from doing some things we may object to in public, but in our homes we can choose to invite in only people who will respect our choices. Therefore, we have an obligation to communicate to our visitors when their actions may be inconsistent with the values we choose to uphold in our homes.

No matter what philosophy, religion, or ethical system we may embrace, if we aspire to grow, mature, and find meaning in our life we must work to bring our behavior more and more in line with our espoused values. If we are successful in these efforts, our attention will naturally be drawn to increasingly more subtle aspects of our lives. Every choice we make, no matter how seemingly inconsequential, either moves us in the direction we wish to go or hinders us in our evolution. Nowhere is this more apparent than in the choices we make regarding our home.

My home is a place in which I can relax. It is the one place in the world where the lifestyle I passionately embrace is the norm. When I fall into bed at night and pull up my thick quilted comforter, I don't want to be covered in the downy feathering of tortured birds. If I sit down in my big easy chair and invite my children onto my lap to talk about treating each other with kindness, I don't want to be sitting upon the tanned preserved skin of a violently killed and dismembered cow. When my daughter peruses the cabinets and refrigerator looking for a snack, I can be comfortable with her choice, knowing that it still falls within my guidelines of being healthy, wholesome, and humane. My home is my sanctuary. The products that gain entrance to my sanctuary do so by conscious choice. This gives me a little oasis in the world, where my values set the tone. The deed shapes the heart. For our children, our conscious choices begin with the food we serve, the clothes they wear, the soaps and lotions they put on their bodies, and then go further—to the artifacts that shape their minds: toys.

Guns

Most people are aware of the debate over toys that have something to do with battle. As a child, I occasionally played with squirt guns and I see no evidence it made me violent. In college (and I'm not proud to admit this), I even played the game "assassin," which lasts for weeks and involves "hit men" assigned a target to stalk and shoot with a toy gun. However, at the times in my life when I participated in such pretend violence, I'd never fathomed that some day sick individuals might shoot up classrooms of children. Video game technology was not so advanced as to allow its "virtual" violence to seem so realistic. Movies and popular music glorifying weapons were not so pervasive. The days when I played these games were also before I recognized how much the military-industrial complex influences the level of violence in the world. Things are different now. It is becoming more and more evident that all the factors I mention above are desensitizing us to violence and suffering, and paving the way for increasingly extreme actions from demented individuals.

In the context of what is happening around the world, therefore, using toy guns exhibits insensitivity to the victims of weapons violence. It communicates to others that guns are something we approve of. The fact is also that war games glorify violence. If I buy toy guns for my children or allow them in my home, I am in essence condoning their use and not living consistently with my values.

In the heat of the summer, therefore, instead of squirt guns my children have squirt bottles. We managed to live in this society for almost four years before exposure to toy guns at someone else's home forced me to explain to my daughter what guns are. Up until that point, I censored our library books and excluded ones with pictures or text that included guns and killing. I wanted my children to be free of such mental pollution as long as possible. However, once faced with explaining guns, I also explained that I didn't approve of playing with toy guns because real guns were for killing. I told my older daughter that guns caused a lot of suffering in the world and that making them into toys makes us forget how awful they are. She has accepted my view on this and it has never been an issue.

Some people have told me that they, too, felt this way about guns until they found their little boy picking up a stick and saying,

"Pow! Pow!" After that, they figured that not allowing toy guns was not stopping violent play, so they went ahead and bought them. However, I feel there is a big difference between a toy gun and a stick. When a toy gun is set down it still says "gun." Its presence is likely to inspire make-believe that includes violence. A stick on the other hand says "gun" only when the child is actively using it as such. The minute he sets it down, it says "stick." When another child picks it up, it will become whatever her or his imagination dreams up.

When my children and their playmates were smaller and more sheltered, I chose to ignore the occasional imaginary transformations of sticks to guns. I didn't want to draw more attention to this issue and I knew that, because as a group our children had little media exposure, such play usually evolved into something else pretty quickly. To intervene in the private realm of my children's imagination seemed overly intrusive. Instead, I set limits on the real material stuff consistent with my values, and let them choose their make-believe as long as no one was getting hurt. Occasionally, if I was really uncomfortable with the direction their play was going, I might casually bring out a craft and invite the children to do it, thus redirecting their play to something more in line with our values.

However, as our children and their playmates have grown, we have had to take a more active role in dissuading violent play. As the children in our sheltered playgroup mixed with media-saturated children in their neighborhoods, churches, and schools they were increasingly imitating the violent play of their more mainstream peers. When this began to happen, I could see that the aggressive acting-out of children who themselves were probably trying to exorcise the violent themes they'd absorbed from less-sheltered children necessitated a change in structure of our house rules. I now intervene in any play at our house that involves guns, swords, fighting, or killing. I tell the children that these things cause suffering in the world, that I do not approve of them, and that such play is not allowed at our home. So far, I've never had to say this more than once with any particular guest.

While it is easy to recognize the harm of violent play, with other toys it is not so obvious how they contribute to unhealthy behaviors and values.

Barbie Dolls

When I was growing up I had Barbie dolls. I remember vividly making clothes and furniture for them and, years before I had children, I saved a lot of my Barbie stuff, intending to pass it along to them. As I grew older, I came to see Barbie in a very different light. I came to realize that Barbie's entire life revolved around how she looked and what she had acquired. Barbie, I felt, was a highly commercialized plastic entity that drew children into buying all sorts of other things, and that she encouraged a fondness for mass-produced, highly commercial products.

Barbie dolls can't wear normal shoes because their feet are made to wear only heels, and Barbie's proportions are totally unrealistic. The Barbie doll promotes an unhealthy ideal of how women should look—indeed, some psychologists feel that Barbie dolls contribute to unrealistic body-shape ideals and eating disorders in girls and young women. When my then four-year-old received her very first Barbie doll as a gift, I was mortified! None of her friends had any and before this gift my daughter was clueless as to Barbie's existence—I'd hoped to keep it this way as long as possible. I figured it was much more appropriate to foster a preschooler's interest in mothering and diapering soft dolls than it was to encourage her to play with a sexualized, difficult-to-dress, plastic, and consumption-focused Barbie.

The day Barbie made an appearance at our house I ran down to the basement, where I keep a stash of toys that my children don't have access to, and brought up armfuls of interesting stuff and placed it in my daughter's bedroom. Once my daughter was absorbed with the other toys, I discreetly moved Barbie to the top shelf of my closet and waited to see if my daughter would notice. Several days passed, and I rotated the toys in my daughter's room back to the basement and brought up some new stuff. A week passed, and there was still no request for Barbie. Finally, several months later, prompted I am sure by seeing a Barbie somewhere else, my daughter finally asked what ever happened to "that doll."

By this time there had been a number of changes in the toys that were out for her to play with. I nonchalantly told her I hadn't seen the doll in a while. "It probably was put in storage when some of the new toys were put out," I told her. That was the last time she ever asked about it. Realizing that this would probably not be our last encounter with Barbie, I took a tip from some friends whose children were much older. Instead of prohibiting Barbie, they turned the doll into a joke. The parents made fun of how weird Barbie's body was, how inappropriately it was dressed, and how there was just far too much pink in everything associated with it. In fact, at the toy store, the parents shielded their eyes from all the bright pink on the Barbie aisle—and their daughters followed suit!

I have tried this with my daughter too and it seems to be working. It's a good thing too, since Barbie has turned up a few more times in other places. Now my daughter just laughs and calls Barbie silly. Someday, when my children are old enough to understand my concerns with this toy, I may give my old Barbies to them. I will do so, however, in the context of sharing with them a toy from my childhood. We won't buy anything for the dolls but instead *make* things—if they're interested.

Electronic Toys

We have also largely avoided electronic toys and things requiring batteries. We've found that the more simple a toy is, the more it invites a child to use her imagination—and the more possibilities exist for utilizing it in whatever she is doing. I look at the intellectual growth of children as in some ways mirroring the growth of knowledge in humankind. We didn't start out utilizing electricity and microchips, and nor should children. It makes the most sense to me to allow my children to develop a solid experience-based understanding of the basic laws of the natural world before starting to explore electronics and higher technology like computers—all more recent discoveries.

I believe that toys that allow exploration of spatial relationships, sensory differences, water, air, gravity, and vibration, along with coordination-building equipment, art supplies, and soft dolls, are all a child really needs for the first seven or eight years. Children who have too much exposure to electronic toys are likely to find lower-tech stuff boring and miss out on the benefits that come only after extensive exploration with things like blocks, marbles, spinning tops, and various other types of constructive and connective items. There are also many electronic toys which, if held too close to a child's ears, can damage her hearing, so loud are they!

As much as possible, I try to find toys that are wooden rather than plastic, which is derived from non-renewable resources like fossil fuels. Some plastics contain chemicals known as endocrine disrupters that in unbelievably minute amounts can interfere with our hormonal systems (and may be a factor in the increasingly younger age at which puberty begins). Wooden toys feel good to touch and vibrate "quality." Unpainted, unvarnished wood carries the lowest risk of introducing undesirable chemicals into the mouths of teething babies. While a room filled with plastic toys has an unsettling effect, a room filled with wooden toys is calming.

Although wooden toys tend to be more durable, finding them can be a challenge. For the most part, mass marketers of toys carry very few wooden items. However, a number of mail-order companies (see Resources) carry a wonderful selection. Unfortunately, because these toys are often labor-intensive and made for a much smaller market, they can be pricey. When relatives anxious to spend money on our children ask what they can buy us, I hand them one

of these catalogs. By ordering wooden toys from mail-order companies we are also supporting small, sometimes home-based business-
es rather than multinational corporations.

Even so, it is very rare that I actually buy new items from either
these companies or the retailers. The vast majority of toys we've
acquired come from garage sales and second-hand shops. I've
explained to my children that buying things this way makes our
money go farther and means that Daddy can work less and spend
more time with us! Although plastic toys far outnumber wooden
ones at these places, when wooden toys do turn up they are usually
priced lower because the average buyer is looking for plastic!

With toys, I believe in the general rule that less is more. A room
full of play items can overwhelm a young a child and make it less
likely he or she will focus on any one toy for very long. The child may
think that he's fully explored everything when he's barely focused
upon any one item more than briefly before becoming distracted and
moving on to another. Every time I acquire new toys I place them in
a special storage area in the basement that is off limits to the children.
Every few weeks (or whenever I am desperate for time to myself), I
bring a few items out of the storage area and add them to the playroom, and several toys from the playroom go back into storage. This
usually buys me a few hours to work on my own projects without
much interruption and it keeps the mess in the playroom to a man-
ageable level that my children can clean up all by themselves.

Avoiding Mass-Marketed Products

As a child I remember loving anything associated with Walt Disney.
However, that was thirty years ago and a time when the main things
associated with Disney were movies, stories, and Disneyland. Today,
the Disney product line is far more extensive and tirelessly marketed.
Disney and other mass-appeal characters promote the full gamut of
consumerism in an ever-increasing number of media venues. Toys,
dolls, figurines, sports equipment, bath accessories, linens, office and

school supplies, and even junk food are promoted to children by exploiting their fondness for specific fictional beings. Some of these figurines, such as Pocahontas, are highly sexualized, and thus inappropriate for young children. Moreover, the popular themes in Disney (and other movies) tend to reinforce stereotypes.

Of most concern to me, however, is that exposure to these mass-marketed characters serves to prime children to be consumers of whatever the advertisers are hustling. I have attempted to shield my children as much as possible from every organization—whether Disney, Barbie, or *Sesame Street*—and any character whose name and likeness is being used to sell merchandise to children.

As you can imagine, this has not been easy. Almost every family member and non-family adult friend outside our beloved playgroup doesn't understand why we eschew these characters. They believe we're depriving our children of the joy of childhood. But we feel that we are allowing them to have a childhood—free of advertisers who see our children not as precious developing beings but as consumers in the making who need to be trained, groomed, and influenced in order to best benefit the corporate world's bottom line.

This lack of understanding is perhaps especially so in the very oldest of today's citizens—the generations who grew up during the Depression. They have a very hard time understanding how the problems facing many families today have nothing to do with a lack of material goods but with having *too much*! However, since we don't watch television or videos, or go to the movies, my girls' only exposure to these mass-marketed items has been through books, little trinkets, or stuffed animals. This has kept the fictional characters' seductiveness at a fairly minor level. I also have further toned down the influence of this merchandise by not encouraging the name recognition of the mass-marketed toys that have found their way into my children's hands.

For instance, the stuffed *Sesame Street* character Big Bird that a relative gave my daughter I referred to as the "yellow doll." It was probably a full year later before she ever realized that nearly everyone else called it Big Bird and that it had a set personality, life, and friends. By then, however, her imagination had already given the yellow doll an identity uniquely created by her.

Turning Off the Television

Perhaps the most significant item in most homes that influences our children's values and behavior is television. In her book *Shelter for the Spirit: How to Make your Home a Haven in a Hectic World*, Victoria Moran, in making her case for turning off the television, points out how it might not be all bad. There are some educational shows and even a few dramas with uplifting themes. But then she asks her readers a telling question: "Is that how you use TV?"

Let me confess: I am a television addict. Fortunately, I'm now celebrating almost five years of sobriety. It wasn't easy at first; yet the longer I go without using television to "relax," "unwind," or "veg out," the more clearly I can see how damaging and negative the medium is. While some people can sit in a room with a television on and carry on a conversation, I cannot. Unless I deliberately don't look at the television set, I find myself drawn into the most inane things. Whatever comes on—whether it's a commercial or a show—grabs me: I must know more. It took a very conscious choice and a strong commitment on my part to free myself from the clutches of this machine.

As with many other life changes brought on by becoming a mother, my liberation from the "plug-in drug" began with the birth of my first baby. At that time my husband and I had a little ritual we shared. Starting years before he met me, my husband had watched the daytime television soap opera *Days of Our Lives* with one of his college buddies. Later, he and his friend, now living in different cities, continued to watch this show, recording it during the day and replaying it in the evenings. For them, in addition to being an addiction, the show was a shared experience evoking memories of camaraderie and carefree days. During telephone calls, whenever he spoke with this friend, I would hear him touch base about the latest crisis on *Days*.

Up to the point my husband and I met, I'd had no interest in the daytime soaps—although through my own college days I had religiously stayed home on Friday nights to watch the evening soap opera *Dallas*. Even then, I was vaguely aware there was something sad about a young single coed choosing to spend Friday evenings with fictional relationships (and very negative ones at that) rather than real people. When my husband and I started to spend time together, we began to watch his soap opera. In no time at all I was hooked—even while I openly criticized the rampant negativity.

I immediately felt something was wrong. Every time an episode ended, I could feel a cloud over my head. The betrayals, jealousy, hatred, and small-mindedness exhibited by the characters lingered in my thoughts almost as much as if people I really knew and cared about were behaving that way. In my real life for some time I'd made a conscious choice to surround myself with people I could trust and who would inspire me to be my best self. It baffled me that I would allow myself to be dragged down by this fictional world.

What made matters worse was that after watching our soap opera together we would be too immobilized to come up with something better to do. Often we would flip channels, trying to find something else to watch. Inevitably, our inertia would take us to the nightly news programs, where our brains could finally be fully saturated with the very worst experiences of humanity. Then, feeling mentally polluted and lethargic, we'd turn the television off and call it a day. In the dark, I would think: "Another wasted night."

For the first few months as new parents we continued this comfortable ritual, during which time I felt doubly guilty as I contemplated the impact of all the negativity upon our new baby. Even though we knew our baby was preverbal and couldn't comprehend the evil the television was spouting, we also knew that babies are virtually all sensation—literally soaking up vibrations. We decided not to watch television anymore when our baby was in the room, relegating it to the time when she was asleep.

But that was only the beginning of my realization of the problems with television. As I thought through all the images on television, both those depicted on commercials as well as those shown as part of the setting for the myriad other shows, I saw that in essence television was depicting a particular way of living I didn't agree with. Since I was working to find role models for my children who could positively reinforce the examples my husband and I were setting, I wondered why I would want to allow anonymous others into my home to set an example of how to live in a manner entirely contrary to the values we were teaching.

I started to think more about television and its impact upon families, and more specifically upon children. When I was watching television, I began to notice more of the nuances. Everywhere I looked on television were babies drinking formula and not sucking on a breast. So many of the commercials were for food, and over ninety-nine percent of the food was not something we ate. Another large group of commercials were for medications—and showed that the way to solve any ailment, no matter how small, was to take drugs. Most people on television were slender and gorgeous (in spite of the wretched diet they were promoting) and had become so because of the cornucopia of cars, toys, makeup, clothing, and other stuff they owned. If they weren't happy, it was either because someone had done something bad to them or because they lacked some material item. These were not the role models I wanted for my children.

At that point I realized that I didn't want my young children to watch television—*at all*. I also realized that the only way I could possibly make this happen was if I, too, never watched television. I knew I had to set the example for them that not watching television was normal and a good way to live. I formally announced to my husband that I would henceforth not be watching any more television and, while I could not persuade him to let me get rid of the set, I did manage to convince him to move the television to a remote area of our home (it now sits in a windowless room in our basement). Of all the non-mainstream choices we have made, this is the one our families have challenged the most.

I will go further in my challenge to convention. Even if television showed only programs and advertisements that fully reinforced our lifestyle and were educational, I would still not want my children to watch it. Most parents intuitively know there's something unhealthful about the medium itself. It mesmerizes us, and especially children. That's why parents use it! It completely occupies their children so they can get a little time to themselves. Many of the mothers I've talked to tell me they can just "feel" that the television is doing something to their children's brains, and they're right.

According to research by Jane Healy Ph.D., shows like *Sesame Street* "anesthetize" higher brain functions. Advertisers and producers of children's television know that increasingly more intense sights and sounds are necessary to keep children's brains from habituating (going to sleep) to the stimuli of television. To counter this, the advertisers and producers increase the frequency of new images and introduce jarring stimuli. Although this keeps children's attention, it creates a stressful situation in their body by releasing hormones and chemicals associated with the fight or flight response. Marie Winn, author of *Plug-in Drug*, suggests that parents tend to overestimate the benefits of *Sesame Street*, partly because of the enthusiasm of other parents and partly because it increases recognition of numbers and letters even though there is no evidence of this leading to general cognitive development. By not allowing enough time for reflection and response, fast-paced shows like *Sesame Street* predispose children to have a short attention span and crave rapid change in order to stay interested in their environment. In the final analysis, *Sesame Street* is nothing more than entertainment, which mainly teaches children one thing: the habit of watching television.

Another such show is *Teletubbies*. I came across them by chance, thumbing through a news magazine article describing their popularity in the United Kingdom. The photos of these cuddly little characters with televisions in their bellies and antennae on their heads seemed alarmingly Orwellian. The idea of merging the mind-numbing technology of television with a soft, lovable creature, and then specifically targeting a group of children younger than had ever been targeted before I found revolting. It seems sinister to create such a character as a Teletubbie. No doubt some children exposed early on and encouraged to identify with *Teletubbies* will be "primed" for a life centered on television. I pity them.

While some would argue that a little bit of television-watching every once in a while probably won't prime a child for life, I would counter that the medium is very seductive. I'm also saving myself the aggravation of dealing with my childen's endless requests to watch the thing. For a young child, every moment spent watching television is robbing her or him of the kinds of activities that promote brain growth, creativity, and coordination. I fully recognize that as my children grow older I will need to relinquish control in more and more areas. But, right now, I can orchestrate and structure so much without them even realizing I'm doing it—let alone them objecting to it.

This has immense benefits for them and our entire family. Because we have carefully chosen which aspects of the larger culture to allow into our lives, our children are not jaded. Everything is new and exciting to them. When our children really want and need more freedom to explore the world, we'll be able to loosen the reins and still be in relatively wholesome territory.

Television, Videos, and the Extended Family
We made ourselves very clear to both sets of grandparents (for all of whom television figures very prominently in their lives) and specifically told them that when our children were visiting, we didn't want them in the same room as any television that was turned on. We

asked them to let us know if they felt compelled to watch television when their grandchildren were visiting; if so, we would be happy to come and get the children and take them home with us. We also made sure they understood that our feelings about television extended to videos—even educational ones. On several occasions both sets of grandparents have crossed the line on this one. Since visits with grandparents are only about three hours per week, I find it incredible that they've felt compelled to show our kids videos against our wishes. Other relatives have warned us that our children's verbal abilities will suffer if we "deprive" them of *Sesame Street*, or that we won't possibly survive parenthood if we don't use the television to get some breaks. All of the pressure just makes me feel like a non-user surrounded by addicts!

To my dismay, my husband, a sports fanatic, still watches basketball and football on television. He does this in the television dungeon and occasionally the children have wandered in to where he is. So far, they've shown little interest in the games, and my husband changes the channel to ice-skating or golf when the commercials come on. Often I will attempt to get them interested in an activity outside that basemant room. I'm hoping that my example on this will prevail over my husband's.

There is one exception to our rule of no television or video exposure for our children. We do, every once in a while, allow them to watch videos of themselves that I've taken with our video camera. Interestingly, even this has demonstrated to me how addictive the medium is. While my five-year-old has never asked to watch television *per se*, for about a week following any time I do watch a home video with her, I get at least one request each day from her to watch more. The majority of the time I simply say, "No." However, every once in a while, when I really need the break, I will set her up with thirty to forty minutes' worth of home video footage. As testament to the medium's ability to mesmerize and influence, this is one of the few times I can guarantee that my daughter will not come ask me for anything! But here's what I find really disturbing: Something that she was doing in that video will become the predominant theme in her play for about four or five days afterwards.

Once, after I purchased a new kitchen appliance and I wanted to learn how to use it, I went to watch the video instructions that came with it. My five-year-old followed me to the basement. While we watched two strangers demonstrate the appliance and describe what to do, my daughter seemed very perplexed. She got very serious and said to me, "Are they talking to us?" Even after having watched me take and replay hours of our own video footage, and even after I explained to her that these people were only talking into a video camera, and that they had done this some time ago, she still seemed to have difficulty separating the present reality from what was on the tape. For me, far from showing how television can help in getting children to separate reality from fantasy, this incident shows just how vulnerable and open children's minds are to persuasion. I'd rather their imaginations were more flexible and self-determined before they're exposed to such a powerful medium. While many have tried to argue that television is not very influential, it seems incredible that advertisers would collectively spend many billions of dollars each year on television spots to influence people if it wasn't.

The Passivity of Television

The problems with television extend beyond only the content— which may include violence, sexism, irresponsible sexual behavior, materialism, unhealthful food choices, and negativity—to the medium itself. When children watch television, they are seduced into behaving in an unusually passive manner. Passivity is not a healthy state for children. Their brains require motor involvement for the building of new neural connections.

In his exceptional book *The Four Arguments for the Elimination of Television*, former advertising agency partner Jerry Mander makes a compelling case that the medium itself is the problem. He argues that television (like a weapon of mass destruction) is not a neutral technology and that the technology itself predetermines who will use it, how they will use it, how it will affect people, and, most important, the sorts of political structures it will ultimately lead to. Although Mander wrote the book over twenty years ago, his description of how television—in its visual effects, rapidity of scene changes, and violence—necessarily evolves to become more intense in order to remain interesting to the viewer is truer now than ever.

One more aspect that must also be considered while contemplating television is the physiological effect of radiation upon the brain and eyes. In his landmark work *Health and Light*, published in 1973, John N. Ott details experiments that deserve further investigation regarding the effects of television on our health. Alarmingly, Ott describes how the pigment granules of the retina's epithelial cells, which have no known function, are highly stimulated by a television tube, even when covered by a photographic paper that prevents passage of all visible light. Ott suggests that such stimulation may affect the pineal or pituitary glands and have an impact upon the endocrine system.

For most people, television is so much a part of their lives they cannot fathom living without it. It is my fervent hope that family after family will decide to remove this powerful, destructive influence from their lives. Television is nothing more than a direct conduit of influence from the world's most powerful corporations to the minds of us, the consuming masses. Television creates and affects our reality in ways so subtle that the average viewer is completely unaware of what is happening.

If you don't believe how brainwashed or addicted you are to television, I challenge you to abstain totally from watching it for six months. After the inevitable withdrawals and anxiety, you'll experience having more time, more energy, and a more positive outlook. You may never go back.

Movies

While my husband and I do occasionally watch movies, we've never taken our children to one and we do not show them commercial videos. For young children, movies are very over-stimulating—both visually and aurally. The previews and advertisements for movies and on videos are even worse—I often feel assaulted by them myself. Instead we take our children to live children's theater and dances. These things are much easier for them to recognize as "fantasy."

By way of confirming I'm on the right track, I've never seen intense excitement in my older daughter for any of the mass-marketed characters (as I so often do with children raised in the mainstream). While she may express fondness for Winnie the Pooh or Madeline stories, what really gets my older daughter excited is a homemade scavenger hunt, building things in the snow, or the prospect of jumping in a newly raked-up pile of leaves—all things that no one can sell to her and don't take a toll on the natural world.

Having Fun: Toys and Roughhousing

I expect my children to entertain themselves a good part of each day—and they do. The majority of their time is spent in make-believe: "House," "Tornado," "Gardening," "Farmer's Market," "Going to the Moon," and "Trip" are a few of the scenarios they like to play. They also love to build structures out of pillows, blankets, boxes, and chairs. My five-year-old loves to play board games too. And many days, we have a period of family "roughhousing." It's our answer to finding a game that's fun for two adults, a five-year-old, and a one-year-old. Sometimes we just chase, tickle, and wrestle, sometimes our fun evolves around throwing and catching a ball, other times we play hide-and-seek.

Our toy collection includes many different types of wooden blocks, including the amazingly versatile Kapla blocks. We have dolls and stuffed animals, and a cardboard puppet theater. We have Lincoln Logs—the old-fashioned ones made of wood. We have puzzles, magnifying glasses, kaleidoscopes, gyroscopes, prisms, and magnets. We have Lego. We have miniature wooden cars, boats, trucks, and trains. We have a toy kitchen with pots and pans and a real ceramic tea set. We have sand and water toys (and a sandbox and plastic wading pool), musical instruments, bikes, scooters, and lots of arts and crafts supplies. And best of all, the vast majority of everything we've acquired came from garage sales and second-hand shops.

From large cardboard boxes I've created playhouses and a space shuttle for indoor play. Outside, made entirely from leftover wood scraps from a neighbor's newly built home, I created two tree houses equipped with tin-can telephones and pulleys. Our children have a lot to play with, and I defy anyone to say they're deprived of stimulation or fun! Yet, the toys we have encourage problem-solving abilities, acquaint them with the basic laws of physics, build their creativity, and have cost our family next to nothing. By selecting or creating the toys we have, while limiting our children's exposure to electronics, television, and other media, we model to our children the joy and satisfaction of thriftiness and resourcefulness, and postpone, we hope indefinitely, the mind-numbing and thoughtless influence of corporate greed upon our children.

Chapter Eight
Education

I HAVE ALWAYS LOVED THE MONTESSORI PHILOSOPHY OF education. It's what I experienced as a young child. My mother's passion for Montessori led her to train as a teacher and, over the course of thirty years, establish and direct two different Montessori schools. When she was fresh out of medical school, Dr. Maria Montessori, Italy's first woman doctor and a pioneer in the education of young children, founded an educational establishment when she was assigned a group of children who were developmentally delayed and considered "uneducable."

Montessori
At first Montessori simply observed the children and recorded her observations, but her philosophy evolved as she attempted to make sense of what she saw. Next, she created beautiful materials specifically to fulfill the children's developmental needs. Her approach was incredibly successful. Children previously labeled "uneducable" began meeting or surpassing their "normal" peers. Dr. Montessori became an important mentor to the famous child psychologist Jean Piaget, whose scientific demonstrations form the basis of much of what is known about the developmental phases of childhood.

So popular are Montessori's ideas around the world that there's nothing that keeps virtually anyone from opening up a school—no matter its philosophy, how the teachers are trained, or whether it even has the special materials—and calling it "Montessori." This has led to a tremendous variety of interpretations of what Montessori is, and misunderstandings abound. Because the Montessori approach has been so successful at educating children, often exceeding expectations, many people mistakenly think that the purpose of Montessori education is to produce academically gifted children.

The purpose of Montessori, however, is really self-actualization. (Montessori used the term "normalize.") This is accomplished through what Montessori termed the "cycle of activity." She discovered that if a child was allowed to select his own work and carry it through to completion the work was like therapy for his soul. She felt that children would often select the activity most likely to facilitate this, if they were given freedom within a highly structured environment to do so. Montessori always referred to a child's activities as "work," not because it was drudgery but so that adults would recognize the importance to the child of whatever activity he had selected and give it due respect. Play is the child's work.

If you visit a good Montessori classroom, you'll be amazed at what happens. Children arrive at the beginning of the morning with their energy scattered, some perhaps nursing emotional upsets from things that may have happened at home. Then, after a period of "work" at school, the children start to focus and become absorbed in what they're doing. Their faces light up as they obviously take pride in their work. Learning takes place not for any sort of reward or acknowledgment but simply for its own intrinsic value. Montessori is often quoted as saying, "The adult works to perfect the environment. The child works to perfect himself." I believe this to be true.

The positive effect of this on the children's psyche is obvious. The fact that children in Montessori classrooms tend to be so intellectually advanced is merely a byproduct of the self-actualization that occurs there. "Normalized" children naturally absorb knowledge. Of course, it helps too that the Montessori materials are self-teaching, beautiful to see and touch, and incredibly good at facilitating the neural connections that growing brains are making.

Although as a high school student I audited a Montessori teacher-training program, I don't feel capable of recreating all the parts of a good Montessori classroom in my home. Classrooms usually include an age span of about three years—something that gives opportunities to older children to be "teachers" to the younger ones and the younger children to anticipate getting to do the more advanced activities they have seen the older children do. In addition, a Montessori classroom is highly structured with clear routines. Within this wonderful structure, children are given a great deal of freedom to move about the classroom and select their own activities. In contrast, the routines in my own life repeatedly stymie my determination to follow a project I believe in through to the end!

For this reason, I wanted my children to spend part of their preschool years in a good Montessori classroom. However, parents interested in recreating some of the Montessori materials at home can follow the directions in any of a number of good books available at the library that detail how to make and use Montessori materials.

Waldorf

There is another philosophy of educating children growing in popularity: Waldorf Education, based upon the writings and philosophy of Rudolf Steiner. Steiner was a brilliant man who lived about the same time as Dr. Montessori. Steiner's interests and contributions to the world were remarkable and he is commonly credited with being one of the founders of organic gardening.

I have never actually visited a Waldorf elementary classroom, but I have seen a video of one, read about them, and spoken with parents whose children have attended them. I have, however, observed a Waldorf preschool that my daughter attended. There are some similarities and differences between Waldorf and Montessori at the preschool level. Both educate through concrete experiences as

125

opposed to teaching in the abstract. Both are child-centered rather than teacher-centered and tend to attract teachers who are passionate about their work, love children, and consider it a privilege to work with them. Both utilize an exquisitely prepared classroom with beautiful and appealing materials, and both handle discipline largely by redirecting children to appropriate activities, although Waldorf seems to put more emphasis on facilitating positive interactions between the children and working with them to resolve conflicts.

Unlike the Montessori classroom, where the routines encourage children to work independently with the materials, in the Waldorf classroom children are encouraged the majority of the time to interact and play with each other. Both Montessori and Waldorf philosophies emphasize the importance of routine and ritual to children, Waldorf perhaps a little more so. Waldorf also places more emphasis than Montessori on the arts.

What I found most appealing about Waldorf schools is how strongly they promote the sheltering of small children from many of the less wholesome aspects of our culture. The Waldorf school we attended encouraged parents not to expose their children to television, videos, or plastic toys. There was a dress code that prohibited children from wearing any clothing to school with logos, words, or illustrations, and all the food served to the children was plant-based and generally healthful.

There are, however, some profound differences between the systems. Montessori views the developing child as passing through specific "sensitive periods." These are times when the child's brain is primed to learn certain things like walking, talking, reading, etc. For instance, if a child is not exposed to verbal language during the sensitive period for language, learning to talk later on will be much more challenging and an opportunity will have been missed. Recent brain research does indeed suggest that the child's brain, in terms of its ability to master certain things, is filled with open doors that close at predetermined times.

Waldorf, on the other hand views the child as an incarnation of a heavenly being. Much of what is and isn't done in the Waldorf classroom is based upon not wanting to "incarnate" the child's soul prematurely. Consequently, every attempt is made to facilitate fantasy in the young child, while learning to read and other academic pursuits are strongly discouraged prior to the acquisition of the permanent teeth at around age seven. The philosophy cautions that study of academics prior to that age is likely to lead to child burnout.

The Waldorf teacher sees herself as working to facilitate the child's imagination and develop his ability to fantasize and play. Children are encouraged to be "up in the clouds," so to speak. In contrast, Montessori philosophy directs the adults around a child to help him differentiate between fantasy and reality by always encouraging him to participate in real activities rather than fantasy play. Montessorians work to help children be well-grounded.

My Unease with Waldorf

My own experience with the two left me a little uncomfortable with the effect of the Waldorf program on my daughter. Granted, my daughter is extremely imaginative to begin with and has no difficulty playing and pretending—in fact, she loves make-believe. I neither encourage nor discourage fantasy—it's her thing, and for the most part I feel I should respect her choices. I do, however, give her opportunities to join me in real and purposeful activities such as cleaning the floor, watering the plants, food preparation, and so forth.

During her Waldorf days I remember finding it very challenging to do "real" things with my older daughter without her trying to make it into some fantasy game. One day, we were baking together. As she stood on the step stool at the counter stirring a bowlful of ingredients, my daughter looked up at me and said: "Hey, Mom, let's pretend that you are Molly and I am Jenna, and we work in a restaurant...." Her request made me wonder why she felt a need to turn a perfectly wonderful fun and "real" experience into some make-believe game. (Cooking in the kitchen with Mom was a special treat she didn't get to do as often as she would have liked.) To me it was evidence that Waldorf was not helping my child to "be here now." Instead, it was encouraging her to "escape" from reality. Perhaps there are children who have trouble playing and fantasizing and who would benefit from Waldorf rather than Montessori. But, in our situation, the Waldorf approach appeared to encourage an insatiable desire to fantasize and seemed very unbalanced.

I had one other discomfort with the Waldorf program. Something about the stories they told the children or the play things they used seemed to facilitate an acting out of medieval themes that occasionally led to swordfights and other sorts of aggressive play. In general, my sense of the Waldorf philosophy is that it condones and encourages to some extent this type of acting out. It is seen as having a therapeutic benefit for the children by allowing them to work through certain inner issues.

As I understand it, the Waldorf elementary program is quite a bit different than Waldorf at the preschool level. In fact, it seems to have much more in common (philosophically) with Montessori. But since I haven't really known any children who have been in the elementary program, I have no strong opinions about it, although I tend toward seeing it as having advantages over traditional public school education. I have, however, been in Montessori elementary classrooms and been very impressed by what I saw. The students appeared very mature, focused, and respectful of others. They were joyful and excited about what they were learning and seemed to be making tremendous academic progress.

Choosing the Right Schooling for Your Children

When I had my "Animals on Wheels" business and traveled around to preschools, daycares, and elementary schools, I had a chance to observe a wide variety of educational settings. With a few exceptions, the environments in which children were being warehoused saddened me. Children were belittled, humiliated, talked down to, or yelled at to force them to conform to an atmosphere that was rigid and made few allowances for their individual differences. The teaching was this way as well—too often in the abstract and geared to a very narrow "norm" that left the majority of students feeling either bored or lost. The physical environments often were overwhelming, with every bit of wall space taken up by a dizzying assortment of posters, artwork, and even advertising—cleverly disguised as "educational" materials.

In the book *When Corporations Rule the World*, author David Korten writes:

> According to Consumers Union, 20 million U.S. school children used some form of corporate sponsored teaching materials in their classrooms in 1990. Some of these are straightforward promotions of junk food, clothing, and personal care items. For example, the National Potato Board joined forces with Lifetime Learning Systems to present, "Count Your Chips" a math oriented program celebrating the potato chip for National Potato lovers month. NutraSweet, a sugar substitute, sponsored a "total health" program.

I find it very disturbing that advertisers can hawk their products to a captive audience of schoolchildren. That these companies' products appear to be sanctioned by a school—an entity looked up to as an authority by our children and us—makes it even worse. If I were to send my child to public school, I would regularly visit her classroom and help her to consciously recognize the propaganda and its intended purpose, and then I would share information to provide a balancing point of view.

With the demeaning way many children are treated and with the assaults to their senses, no wonder discipline problems in the schools are so severe! I saw the problems firsthand. Indeed, my exposure to so many "traditional" preschools at this time in my life left such a strong impression upon me that when I was considering a preschool for my own daughter, I never even bothered to check a single one of these out.

Speaking from my own experience, I do feel that many toddlers, perhaps more so than preschoolers, have a very strong need to socialize with others and explore novel environments. This need, however, must also be balanced with toddlers' very strong need to have ready access to their mothers when the challenges of life overwhelm their tenuous coping skills. Mother and child playgroups can meet all these needs quite well.

Dedicating Time to Your Children

A common refrain I hear today is from mothers who tell me they cannot remain at home but have to work outside it. Sometimes this is for financial reasons; other times women see working outside the home as critical for their self-esteem. Some women simply think that they would go crazy at home with their children.[1]

Women (and men) are bombarded by the idea that we can and should have it all. I don't believe we can. Life is full of choices. It's clear that mothers should have interests and projects (which can include financial compensation) that aren't focused on their children, so they can maintain their own identity and give their offspring some "breathing room" to develop on their own without being smothered. But it is unfortunate that, as a culture, we encourage parents to leave their children in the care of others while we pursue our work.

This needn't be the case. Children benefit immensely by being in their parents' presence without being the focus of undue attention. Many families have found creative ways to balance their "work" with child-rearing responsibilities. Starting your own business, working at home, caring for other people's children, farming, or splitting shifts with your spouse are some of the ways that families can find the flexibility to earn income and have a focus outside their children—without delegating their parental responsibilities to others.

While new studies abound that supposedly show that children in daycare turn out just fine, these studies do not persuade me. The studies may assuage the guilt of parents who delegate much of the care for their children to others in spite of that small quiet voice inside, but I and other stay-at-home mothers often see noticeable differences in the demeanor, focus, creativity, and self-direction of daycare children. These nuances could mean the difference between a child growing up inclined to follow the pack or one who thinks for himself. Furthermore, the more a child is away from you, the less influence you will have with her. Ask yourself: Whose values do I want my child to adopt?

Because a child under the age of about two and a half to three is not proficient at expressing himself with language, we cannot be sure if something emotionally damaging is happening to that child while in daycare. Of course, there might be signs in his behavior that could indicate the chosen caregivers are not responsive enough or lose their tempers. But a change in your child's behavior could also be a symptom of anxiety in the larger family system (for which you could have a blind spot too) or due to developmental changes in the child. You don't want to make a mountain out of a molehill, but you also could be missing a sign that that particular environment isn't healthy for your child. For this reason I wouldn't put my children in any program that didn't include my presence prior to their being able to tell me effectively with words what they experience in my absence.

Parents must choose for themselves what matters most to them—more stuff or more time with their children. Is parenting a burden, squeezed between times with other adults or time alone, or a wonderful opportunity to build a very unique connection with another, to grow and mature in ways that only parents can, and perhaps in a small way influence the future? I'm not implying that parents making different choices than I don't passionately love their children too; but I am suggesting that cultural pressure upon us is immense! In so many ways we are encouraged, seduced, and led to adopt a lifestyle that separates us from our children—something that's reinforced and condoned everywhere we go. You may have heard (or made yourself) comments such as: "Haven't you left that baby yet?" or, "Isn't Kim amazing—back at work so soon. Having a baby sure didn't slow her down!" or, "You better get him used to a bottle or you'll never have any freedom." It may be hard, but conscious parenting requires that we find a way to really step outside this pervasive cultural paradigm so we can actually have a choice. We must consciously think about the big picture. How will our choices affect our relationship with our children and how will this impact the type of citizens they become?

Of course, none of this is simple. Relationships, skills, and self-determination are all part of a continuum, and each child and family is unique. Your child might thrive in daycare and you may feel that someone else is more capable of nurturing your child than you. You may see yourself making far more important contributions through your job. I simply suggest here that, as parents, we need to ensure that we're really making a choice and that we've thought about whether that choice is consistent with our dreams of the world we want our children to inherit.

My Decision to Home-School

There is a wonderful Montessori school that goes up through the elementary level located about thirty-five minutes' drive from where we live. Several months after the birth of our second child, we sent our older daughter to this school for nine months, going half a day, five days a week. This decision helped me in adjusting to the change of being the mother of two children and also fulfilled my desire for my children to have at least one year in a good Montessori classroom.

I was very pleased with the school, but the long drive persuaded me that one year was enough. Even if the school had been right across the street, however, I probably would not have wanted my child to stay in it as she got older. My main reason is that, in my heart, I wanted to home-school. I'd had children, not to pass off to others to raise, but because I wanted that experience for myself. I firmly believed— and continue to believe—that in order for me to stay a major influence in my children's lives, I need to invest the time guiding them, sharing my values, setting an example, listening to their perspective on life, and helping them grow into competent adults.

All parents home-school—some just do it more then others. One of the things I didn't like about having my child in school five days a week was that I felt it inhibited our ability to take advantage of the educational opportunities that life spontaneously presents. Trips to museums, libraries, parks, socializing with other families whom we consider a positive influence, or even merely following through on something begun at home—all, I felt, suffered.

What I also didn't like about sending my children away to be schooled was that they would be more susceptible to corporate influences. Even though we screened the school we chose carefully and made sure that no movies, videos, or television would be shown, that fast-food companies wouldn't be passing out coupons and freebies to the children, that dairy industry materials wouldn't be utilized to teach "nutrition," that vending machines weren't in the school, and that no other advertising or promotions would be aimed at our child, I knew that probably every other child at that school (and even most teachers) was virtually under assault from the corporate world almost the entire time he or she was not in school. Most children watch television, listen to commercial radio, eat at fast-food restaurants, subscribe to children's magazines full of advertisements, and play with all the mass-marketed toys. Their whole identity of who they are is inseparable from the image that advertisers have fostered in order to sell them products.

Advertising makes children feel as though they've got to have stuff in order to keep up with one another, breeding an atmosphere in which they're taunted for not wearing the "right" brand-name clothing—something that, quite literally, costs their parents dear. As children get past preschool, they start to experience phenomenal pressure to be like everyone else. This is much more obvious in public school children than it is in children who are home-schooled, who tend to expect everyone to be unique individuals. What many people mistakenly refer to as socialization is nothing more then peer pressure, which, thanks to increasingly aggressive marketing strategies, is rearing its ugly face in younger and younger children.

The Issue of Socialization

Let us deal with the issue of socialization and ask who is better socialized. Is it a child in public school, one who is mostly comfortable only with children of roughly the same age, acculturated to like and do mostly the same things? Or is it a child who, because she is home-schooled and involved in the parents' world, has been interacting with children of all ages and adults who are following their own unique life paths? When I have visited families who home-school, their children join the adults in conversation. They show keen interest in what visitors have to say. They seem very at ease interacting with everyone. These same families also tell me that home-schooling families seem to get through the rocky adolescent years with much less difficulty than those with children primarily educated away from home.

In the last year we have experienced our first year (kindergarten) of home-schooling full-time. We also have our daughter enrolled in a recreational gymnastics program and a music program. Because we live out in the country and have no neighborhood of children around, we can influence who her friends are. We schedule special times for get-togethers with the children of our friends—some of whom are vegan and some of whom are home-schoolers like us. Most are sheltered from the corrupting influence of television, but all of them come from families working to make conscious choices rather than just following the cultural norm. Because of this, we are in some major ways, all of us, outside the mainstream. But we are by no means a homogeneous group—for instance, we're of different

134

religions and live at a variety of income levels. In this, my children are getting the message that it is all right to be different.

When we started home-schooling, I sat down with my daughter and asked her what things she thought would be important for her to learn. Together we made a list and I asked her to set goals in various different subject areas. Then we took a calendar, planned out for a month what we would do day by day, and set aside a special time each day to do it. Things went very well for the first two days—my daughter happily sat at our big table and practiced writing her letters. She worked on writing her numbers out to a thousand (that was the goal she set!).

Then, on day three, we hit a glitch. She decided that she didn't want to do this work anymore, and I rigidly insisted that she stay at the table with her work until it was completed. She ended up sitting at that table most of the day—except for meals and potty breaks. What could have taken her less than thirty minutes filled the entire day while she doodled, complained, and acted bored. I was totally demoralized, and spent the next few days (it was the weekend) doing some serious soul-searching. I came to the conclusion that if I wanted my child to view learning as drudgery, I could just as well send her to public school and save myself the struggle. However, one of the main reasons I chose to home-school was so we could study things as they became relevant and exciting. I wanted her to love learning solely for its own sake.

I completely abandoned our old approach (with no complaints from my daughter) and began focusing on the things we were most successful at. She loves being read to and she loves doing experiments, so that's what we do now. At present, we are reading books about archeology, the origins of the number system, famous individuals, and animals. Except for our bedtime reading, we have no set time for these things. Sometimes, my daughter will spontaneously ask a question and so we look up the answer together. Other times, in response to her query, I will try to devise some concrete way of helping her understand a new concept. These things come easily to me—they feel nurturing and they build a warm connection between us. In the process, I realize we are home-schooling.

One of the most inspiring books I have read about home-schooling is written by David and Micki Colfax and is called *Home-Schooling for Excellence*. It describes the experiences of the Colfax family, who entirely home-schooled four sons until they all went to Harvard. Whether you plan on home-schooling or not, I highly recommend you read this book, since it will open your eyes to the state of public education and help you figure out ways to minimize its downsides, should you choose that for your children.

People often ask me if we are going to home-school forever. I assume that they mean until college. (I do plan to home-school myself forever—I love learning!) My plan is to take this experiment one year at a time and evaluate how things are going. While I'm committed to home-schooling my children, I'm also just starting out. I fully expect to get as much of an education as my children, particularly in learning more about myself. Therefore, I am flexible. We can always try something different if we choose.

---

1. Of course, a father could be the primary caregiver instead. I have seen wonderful families where the father assumed this role. However, only mothers can nurse, and since I place such importance upon this I generally envision mothers as the primary caregivers—at least for babies and toddlers.

Chapter Nine
Family and Community

THE DICTIONARY DEFINES "COMMUNITY" AS A UNIFIED body of individuals, a group of people with a common characteristic, interest, or linked by a common policy living together or scattered apart within the larger society. During our lives we are part of many different communities. Our families, religious groups, work environment, clubs, and various other affiliations all represent communities. Humans have always lived and functioned within community. To not do so would deny intrinsic biological and spiritual needs.

I once met an anthropologist who told me that we now know from studying various cultures around the world that humans, like whales, live in "pods." She said that studies show that for good emotional health children require a minimum pod size of fifteen adult role models that they interact with on a regular basis. These can be neighbors, teachers, relatives, friends, or clergy.

Ask yourself who are in your child's pod and whether they reflect your values and are modeling the way you're trying to live. Obviously you won't find fifteen other adults just like you with respect to all the criteria by which you're striving to live your life. You probably won't even find one. But I do think it's important you have several role models for each of the different major choices you're making that set you apart from our larger culture.

Intentional Community

Because my husband and I recognize the persuasive influence of community on individuals, we occasionally contemplate the idea of actually moving to an "intentional community" that can reinforce some of our lifestyle choices and values. There are hundreds of intentional communities located throughout the United States. They may be as small as just a few families or individuals or have as many as several hundred members. Generally they live in some geographical proximity, sharing certain community buildings or even homes. Some are very loosely organized; others have well-defined bylaws and organizational structures. They may govern themselves democratically or consensually. There are infinite variations on all these aspects.

While we find the idea of living as part of an intentional community very attractive, there are none organized around the theme of compassion close to where we now live. Since we are already part of several other communities, all based in our present geographical location, the most important of which is our extended family, we have a strong interest in staying in this area.

Dealing with Your Family

While my husband and I feel very blessed to have both sets of parents alive, well, and involved in our lives, living in the same city with both sides of our family (although probably very beneficial for our children) also presents challenges. Some studies have suggested that within the context of this culture, the optimal geographic distance for grown children with families of their own to live from their parents is about 150 miles. This makes getting together easy enough for regular contact, yet also provides a degree of distance that can help keep that regular contact a little less intense.

Prior to our having children, living so close to all of our families of origin wasn't even an issue. But, as our family grew, this changed and I feel I've learned a lot in this area. I sometimes bemoan the fact that if only I'd known then (before having children) what I know now I might have handled things differently. I just had no clue that embarking on parenthood would bring me face-to-face with patterns and family issues much older than myself. I stumbled along, mistakenly believing that, in terms of the emotional field, working to be a good parent meant only addressing my marital relationship and our interactions with our children. I couldn't have been more wrong.

Naturally, it all started when I was pregnant. With hormones surging through me, I was even less able to stop and think carefully about my steps in the "family dance" than normal. In addition, pregnant women, by virtue of their obvious physical appearance, seem to attract intrusive comments from everyone, no matter how well-meaning—something that probably served to heighten my anxiety.

Members of my family, of course, were not trying to be intrusive (and in fact they really weren't). They were simply concerned about the unusual (to them) choices we were making. What compounded things was the fact I was feeling insecure (despite my extensive research and strong convictions) about making choices that went so against the grain of our culture and even our own families' histories.

On a more subtle level, a number of other issues were playing themselves out as well. Family members were wondering what relationship they'd develop with the newest members of the family (our babies), and were perhaps anxious about the fact we were not following family expectations in the roles played by members of previous generations. For instance, we never left our babies with anyone before they were a year of age.

While, long before giving birth, I'd given a great deal of thought to how I wanted to raise my children, I'd never considered how I would manage relationships with those in my extended family concerning the significant differences in our parenting choices. By the time I realized what an emotional minefield I'd stepped into, I was shoulder deep in very undesirable and entrenched patterns that created distance between myself and other members of my family.

When I look back, I realize that the smart thing to have done would have been to talk with each member of our extended family (while I was still pregnant) about what types of challenges they encountered when raising their own children. I could have asked them how they dealt with their own urge to protect their children from harm and what choices they'd made that were different from those made by other family members. I could have asked them how they'd handled it and if there were any things they wished they'd done differently.

Discussions of these types would have given me insight into what each member of the family was up against. It would have given me some choice about how I wanted to interact with them—instead of reflexively taking rigid polarizing positions. It would have helped me develop compassion for each person instead of feeling threatened by the differences. It would have made other family members feel I valued their experiences and insights rather than shutting them out.

That's what I *should* have done! Instead, I bombarded everyone with medical journal articles trying to impress them with my thorough research. I endlessly challenged their thinking and tried to convince them my view was right. All those times I attempted to explain to them how harmful eating dairy products or taking vaccines or watching television or having hospital births, or whatever the issue of the day, I knew my words were falling on deaf ears. Within seconds of climbing onto my soapbox I could see their eyes glaze over.

But did I stop? Oh no. Spurred on no doubt by my own anxieties regarding family patterns that I was smack in the middle of but mostly unconscious of, I charged on full force. As a result I never convinced anyone of anything and instead created some uncomfortable distance in some very important relationships. Furthermore, my husband and I became the unwitting recipients of an endless stream of emotionally charged (and on the surface unrelated) attacks. These sapped our energy and our serenity, and stressed our family.

Furthermore, if I'd done things differently and really worked to hear and understand the points of view of the extended family, my husband and I might have still set the same firm boundaries, but we wouldn't have left relatives feeling so undervalued and left out. I wish I could have learned to listen to their unsolicited advice or occasionally shown more interest in hearing their perspective than in sharing mine.

Also, there were some things we simply never needed to disclose. For instance, our relatives didn't *need* to know our view on vaccination in order for our choice to be honored. We should have understood that they would have never agreed with us, and knowing we haven't vaccinated our children has merely caused them great anxiety. We should have spared them the grief!

Bowen Family Systems Theory

Bowen Family Systems Theory, the remarkable philosophy and therapy I mentioned earlier, states that you cannot understand the individual without understanding the larger family system of which that individual is a part. In fact, according to Bowen, it is the family not the individual that is the fundamental emotional unit, and family members function reciprocally in response to life's challenges.

To Bowen, the best thing we can do to raise well-adjusted children is to make sure we work on having calm, regular contact with the widest possible number of individuals from our extended families. This helps to bring unconscious family patterns and beliefs to the level of consciousness, where we can start to have a choice about the role we play. It also gives our children many different examples to follow in dealing with the significant issues particular to our family. This type of work is like money in the bank for our descendants. The degree to which we manage the anxiety in our family of origin directly influences the functioning of our children.

Of course, knowing all this and putting it into practice were— as I've discovered so often—two different things. In my own defense, however, I should say I was adjusting to the new roles of wife and mother as best as I could. On top of that, I happen to have an unusual point of view—one that sees cultural norms as part of a large continuum that encompasses raising children with poor health, global suffering, and/or the destruction of the biosphere. It's an ongoing struggle for me to honor my own convictions and still be an active, loving participant in my larger family. In that, I fancy, I'm not much different from many others.

I have come to see that, while I want my children to grow up with values and dietary choices that in one way or another are not those of my entire family, I do value the love and sense of belonging our extended family provides to us. I see this as especially important for my children. So, we have managed to work out some ways to navigate the more challenging aspects and find a balance between the two.

Food, Community, and the Family

As can be imagined, the most challenging aspects for me always revolve around food. I simply cannot turn off my knowledge that the consumption of chicken involves in some way half-smashed baby chicks being carelessly run over by hatchery carts while workers stand by smoking cigarettes. When I see someone drink milk or eat cheese I can't erase the picture of an anemic veal calf in a dark crate unable to turn around—while his mother is enslaved by a mechanical milking machine. I would no more feed my children roasted chicken than road-kill. Needless to say, sitting around a dinner table with people eating animal-based foods makes me nauseated and sad, even though I do it occasionally out of duty and to appease family members whom I'm sure have done the same with me.

There are two holidays, however, that I stand firm on and absolutely refuse to be present at food-based celebrations unless they are vegan. One is Thanksgiving. This is partly because the traditional celebration revolves so particularly around eating an animal, but also because it seems totally hypocritical to be talking about being thankful when we are relishing and consuming a victim for whose suffering and death we are responsible. The other holiday, Passover, is about freedom from enslavement. I cannot celebrate my ancestors' freedom from slavery while looking at dismembered body parts of animal beings that humans continue to enslave.

In order to better deal with this, we have started a tradition of always celebrating Thanksgiving at our house and invite all the relatives to join us. Since everyone knows we don't allow any animal-based foods at our house, this ensures a vegan celebration. We started to do the same thing with Passover, but occasionally a relative will offer to host this instead—and have it be vegan so we can attend.

We are fortunate that our extended family tries to respect our wishes regarding food with our children, and I know this isn't true for other vegan families. If this were the case for me, I'd probably supervise all visits and never leave my children alone with family members who weren't able to uphold our values.

Just as in all aspects of parenting, there are no easy answers for dealing with the extended family. Before you decide on your plan of action, however, I encourage you to give careful thought to how you will proceed. Know what your bottom line is, what ideals you are absolutely committed to, and what you can ease off a little occasionally. Consider how you will go about living your life's principles in a way that is least likely to create anxiety in members of your extended family. Careful attention to this area is well worth the effort

Creating Other Communities
Part of what makes navigating the differences we have with our larger family a little less stressful are the efforts we've made to be part of other communities that model the choices our families don't. These other communities also provide a safe place where we can relax and feel like our conscious (albeit unusual) choices are "normal."

One of these communities is our local vegetarian society. The monthly potlucks and meetings bring us into social contact with others who place a high priority on healthy and compassionate living—and are working to bring their behavior ever more into alignment with this value. We see many of the same friends there every month. A few are vegan. I make sure my children know who they are, so they realize we're not the only vegans in our city. The North American Vegetarian Society (NAVS) and the Vegetarian Resource Group can help you find the vegetarian group closest to you. If there isn't one in your city, these organizations will help you start one.

To make sure we have plenty of other vegans in our lives, we also work to feel a part of the *national* vegan community. Each summer, since the birth of our children, we've gone to the NAVS Summerfest and met dozens of other children who've also been raised vegan. Many times each day while we are there, I take my daughters aside and whisper: "There's Rebecca, Elizabeth, and Nathaniel....They're vegan just like you," or, "There goes Garret—he's a vegan too." This always brings a huge smile to my daughter's face. In fact by the time we return after a week, my five-year-old is beaming, so obviously proud is she of being raised vegan. Summerfest makes her feel part of something special. It's enough to get her through a whole year of politely declining the junk food pervasive in our culture.

Summerfest, however, comes only once a year and our local vegetarian society's potlucks are only monthly, and there are relatively few other families with young children who attend. So we are very fortunate to be part of yet another community: our playgroup.

Creating a Playgroup Community

Prior to the birth of our first child and after we attended the Bradley Childbirth class, the instructor gave my name to a pair of women who had attended one of her other classes and were planning homebirths. They'd approached the instructor, looking for recommendations of new mothers who might be interested in being part of a playgroup. These women were specifically looking for other women who were making some conscious choices in their new role as mothers that might put them outside the mainstream. Their idea was that we could all support each other and help reinforce our commitment to choose those parenting norms we wanted to embrace and those we might avoid in the best interest of our families. My invitation into this community turned out to be an incredible blessing!

The first time I attended playgroup was about six weeks after our first baby was born. At that point, we were all new moms caring for single babies. There were about five families involved at first. Occasionally a family would move or drift away, and from time to time one of us would meet someone new on a similar path and invite her to join us. Playgroup became our little oasis, our study group, our therapy, and our social life. In essence, it was *our* community— one little current pushing us upstream in a raging rapids trying to suck us all down the other way. However, it was enough to keep us all heading in the direction of our choice.

Five years later, there are roughly a dozen families whom we consider part of the playgroup. Most have additional children. Because each family has pursued different activities for the older children, our gatherings are much more irregularly scheduled. We never manage to get everyone together at once anymore and we're hardly as strict as when we started out. Disposable diapers, plastic toys, Barbie dolls, and pacifiers have found homes with some families. We've all, to our own and perhaps others' relief, become a lot less judgmental.

At the outset, my family represented the only vegetarians, let alone vegans. While the babies nursed or played on the floor, we moms would talk. Scientific journals, *Mothering* magazine, various books, newspaper articles—all served as catalysts for mind-expanding discussions about the world and how we saw our newly emerging selves fitting in.

From the outset, we each brought something different to the group. Some mothers were opposed to circumcision; others planned to nurse their babies for three or four years. Some opposed vaccinations; we all shunned daycare, separation of babies from their mothers, formula feeding, and pacifiers. We were all advocates of home-birth, nursing, and the family bed. Some planned on home-schooling; some were into Waldorf, others into Montessori. But beyond all of these daily choices, what we all had in common was a sense that we were not going to mother only the way popular culture suggested we should. Instead, each of us intended to make conscious choices for the benefit of our children and for the future of the world.

From these other families I learned a vast amount. Just as important, however, I felt accepted and supported in my mothering choices. We all did. Our playgroup became a little crucible for alternative mothering, and over time we all influenced each other. Much of what I have written in this book evolved from ideas or literature that my playgroup friends shared with me.

Perhaps my greatest influence on the other families was in the area of plant-based nutrition. We always brought food to share when we gathered and, I presume, out of consideration for my family, the others always brought vegan food. It is a gesture that has touched my heart more than they'll ever know. I've loved having somewhere to go where the food offered reinforced the way we ate at home.

I'm pleased to say that all the mothers are now vegetarian and generally eat very little dairy and eggs, and their children are being raised this way as well. The playgroup parents serve as important role models for my children, but not with respect to every value I hold. So my husband and I emphasize to our children the ones that are similar and we don't apologize for the things they do that we choose not to do. We simply acknowledge the difference and then remind our children that all families are different and that parents have to decide what they believe is best for their own families.

Staying at home with your children can make you feel isolated. Taking a firm stand against the pollution, materialism, and health-destroying and family-compromising aspects of our culture can exacerbate this feeling. A sense of community is essential to our emotional, spiritual, and physical health. Our children not only need to see us feeling connected, but they need opportunities to make their own connections with others distinctive from us. Family and community: We need both to raise healthy, well-adjusted, and compassionate children.

Chapter Ten
Conclusion: Preparing Your Child to Swim against the Tide

T HE FIRST STEP IN PREPARING YOUR CHILD TO SWIM against the tide is to learn to do so yourself. When I was in college studying microbiology, one of my friends who was going through the same program asked me one day: "Doesn't the male chauvinism in this department just drive you crazy?"

"Huh?" I replied. I really didn't have a clue what she was talking about.

"You know," she continued. "The way the guys always get preferential treatment, and all the opportunities." Then she went on to describe to me in vivid detail the many ways that she, because she was a female student, had been slighted.

I've no doubt that those things really happened to her; however, her experience was nothing like mine. Twice during my college career, I'd applied for positions in specific laboratories and twice I'd been selected over all the other applicants, male and female. I always sat in the front row of my large lecture classes and I volunteered frequently to answer or ask questions. I felt acknowledged in class as much as anyone else.

My friend's frustration showed me how different people in the same setting can experience something entirely differently. Whether the differing experiences are due to personality, expectation, or something else, I cannot say. Nevertheless, I realize there can be, so to speak, multiple realities.

Difficulty? What Difficulty?

When we make lifestyle choices outside of the mainstream, I believe the difficulty we encounter because of our choices also varies widely from one person to another. While writing this book, I contacted a number of vegan families I'd not previously known to find out what sorts of difficulty they'd encountered making non-traditional choices. Every single one of them told me that, in essence, they'd never had any serious problems.

I, too, feel the same way. However, I know this can't be true for everyone. I suspect that one's degree of conviction has a lot to do with how one experiences the reactions of others, and whether one's chosen differences become molehills or mountains. Being assertive and able to articulate your point of view clearly makes you less likely to become a target for people looking to impose their way on you. But since I have heard of occasional serious problems that some families have encountered, I am proactive. I do things with an eye to the possibility of keeping myself and my family from being victimized by well-meaning but misinformed others.

From time to time I have heard stories of parental custody being challenged because parents chose not to vaccinate their children, or breastfed "too long," or chose not to give their children dairy products. These stories have come to me more than thirdhand, so I have no idea if there were, intermingled with these families' alternative choices, some things that perhaps did warrant intervention. It is, of course, entirely possible that the families were healthy and were simply targets because they strayed from society's norms.

In any event, the possibility that we could become targets is something I never forget. Even if we were totally vindicated, just the threat of authorities placing a child in foster care for even a few hours would be incredibly traumatic. Because of this, I collect medical journal articles and names of national organizations that promote and support the alternative choices we've made. I have made a special effort to be involved in our community in many ways so that people know us and can vouch for us.

Although we haven't really needed medical care, and I am no fan of "well baby visits," I do take my children in to see our family practice doctor from time to time, for minor concerns. This way, the doctor can see that the children are thriving and can document their good health, and get a sense of who we are as a family. Of course, I always use the opportunity to bring our doctor some of those medical journal articles that he otherwise would probably never see!

Being in Touch with the Larger Community

We work to stay in touch with religious leaders, attorneys, teachers, and others who are well-respected and connected in the larger community. I try to have such individuals over to our home socially so they can see how we really live and get to know my children in their own environment. (They also always get a great sampling of gourmet vegan food!) If ever the concern were raised that we were negligent as parents, we would, therefore, have a large network of articulate and upstanding members of society who can personally attest to the fact we are responsible, loving parents.

Taking a Stand

There have, however, been a few incidents where we have had to go that extra mile to make sure our values were respected by the mainstream. There follow a few instances.

When we sent our daughter to preschool we were forced to address the fact that we don't vaccinate. I looked up my state's law on this issue and saw that if one or both parents are members of a religious denomination whose teachings are opposed to vaccination, they simply needed to state that in writing and provide it to the school in lieu of vaccination records. This I did. Several months into the school year, I received a note from the health department (via our school) requesting to know what religion we were and who our priest was. I was shocked.

Fortunately, I remembered a casual conversation I'd had with an attorney several years previous about the whole issue of religious freedom. He had told me the Supreme Court had ruled that any belief held as dearly as a religious belief qualified as such, and that asking you about your religion and who could vouch for you violated your religious freedom.

Just to be extra careful I called the rabbi who married us and asked him whether it was true that Judaism teaches us to take care of our bodies and not to adulterate them. "Absolutely," he replied.

"Well, rabbi," I said. "I have done an awful lot of research on childhood vaccines, and I believe passionately that they damage the immune system. Would it then be a violation of Judaism's teachings for me to vaccinate my child?"

"Yes," he said. "If that is what you believe." Then we talked about some of the evidence I had uncovered and he requested that I send it to him, which I did.

Next, I drafted a letter to the employee of the health department, who had inspected the school and was inappropriately pressuring us. I attached a photocopy of the relevant state statutes and pointed out how we had complied with the letter of the law. I reiterated my statement that we were adherents of a religious denomination whose teachings were opposed to vaccination. However, I neither stated our religion nor wrote anything else I knew the law didn't require. Then I asked the health department employee to tell me who in the health department had authorized her to invade my family's religious privacy. I gave the letter to my child's teacher to pass along to the health department inspector.

That was the end of it. I never heard another word about it. I can only imagine that my letter made its way up the chain of bureaucracy until an attorney got hold of it and educated the health inspectors about what they legally can and cannot ask parents.

Feeling strong in your convictions and being willing to stand up for yourself make it less likely that you will become a target of some overzealous bureaucrat. Bureaucracy tends to pursue unassertive people. It also helps if you've done your homework and know the laws and can articulate the facts to support your decisions.

Almost three months after our second daughter was born at home, I received a phone call from a nurse in the state capital who was going over the records we had submitted to register our baby's birth and get a birth certificate. She'd noticed there was no record of us having had our newborn tested for PKU, a genetic disorder that leads to mental retardation unless treated. According to Robert Mendelsohn M.D., author of the wonderful book *How to Raise a Healthy Child in Spite of Your Doctor*, PKU is so rare, the test so inaccurate, and the dietary treatment so obnoxious and of such questionable benefit that he advises not doing the test and just breast-feeding your baby—something he feels will offer the child the best hope of health in any event.

Most state laws mandate that hospitals must test all babies at birth for PKU, unless parents refuse the test and sign a waiver. The ridiculous thing about this mandate is that when the baby is less than forty-eight hours old, the results from this test are highly inaccurate. Since most babies leave the hospital prior to this time, the test is largely meaningless. With our firstborn, we refused the test at the time and then brought her back at one week of age. The technician pricked my daughter's heel and then squeezed a few drops of blood out.

It was very traumatic. Our first week, postpartum had been quite peaceful, with very little crying. While her heel was being squeezed my daughter let out a blood-curdling scream that kept going. The technician had to squeeze and squeeze her little heel because she didn't bleed very well. Her extreme distress was very upsetting for me and I started crying. My husband, a few feet away, watched us both and his eyes filled with tears as well.

Later, someone told me that PKU, being genetic, also has some physical characteristics that can be suggestive of it as well—such as light-colored hair and very pale complexion, almost to the point of looking albino. I have since found confirmation of this fact in the *Merck Manual*. The incidence of PKU is about one in ten thousand live births. Based upon all this, plus not wanting to take our new-born into a potentially infective hospital, we decided against doing this test at all.

Therefore, when the nurse called to ask if we had ever had the PKU test done, I was caught completely off guard. The nurse proceeded to tell me how devastating the disease could be. So I said to her, "Isn't it true that the incidence of the disease is about one in ten thousand?"

"Well, yes," she admitted, "but I used to work at a children's hospital and I have seen the babies who weren't diagnosed in time, and it is such a tragedy. However, if it's caught early, and they are given a diet free of phenylalanine, then they are usually all right."

"You have seen some babies who had it?" I asked.

"Yes, I have."

"Well, I heard that you can tell which babies might have PKU because they are almost albino-looking. Is this true?"

"Oh, I don't remember what the babies looked like," she said. "It was a very long time ago."

"Well, at what age would symptoms appear if a baby has it?" I asked.

"By about three months, the developmental delays become obvious," she said. "But by then some damage has been done. The diet must be started before then." (Vegan diets tend to be lower in phenylalanine anyway.)

"My baby is almost that age now," I replied. "She is very alert and responsive, has good head control, and can see and respond to my smile from way across the room. We already have one healthy child, and no known cases of PKU anywhere in our extended families. We had the test for our first child and it was very traumatic. Considering everything, we opted not to put our second child through it."

That pretty much was the end of our conversation. I think this nurse was genuinely concerned about us and called expecting to "educate" us about the dangers of PKU. When she found that I knew the actual incidence of the disorder, and that we had considered the risks in light of our own family histories and made an informed choice, she realized we were not uneducated, lazy, or neglectful, and left us alone.

Fostering Conscious Souls—Yours and Your Children's

Finally, I'd like to offer some thoughts about preparing your child to go out into the world and survive—*happily*—in a culture that abhors nonconformity. While I believe strongly that one of *our* fundamental jobs as parents is to teach our children to think for themselves, I also believe it is just as important to instill our values in them as well. One of my friends told me she was uncomfortable with the idea of influencing her kids to adopt her values, since she wanted them to learn to think for themselves and form their own opinions.

While I agree that children should be taught to think for themselves, I disagree that by influencing our children we are impinging upon their free thought. Children need a firm set of values starting out, to give them structure as well as a clear sense of who they are. Do you throw your child into deep water to teach him to swim or start him out slowly, learning some basics? Furthermore, we do not live in a vacuum. As I have outlined in this book, many powerful entities certainly have no qualms about trying to influence our children to adopt *their* values, and, if we are not clear and convincing, our children will hardly have an alternative choice. Unless we continuously reinforce our values—tell our children why we are doing what we do—then we are leaving our children with no life vest in the insidious riptide that is enveloping our culture.

Some would argue that we shouldn't paddle upstream, that forcing our children to be too different is cruel. This argument is without merit. No matter how we try to convince ourselves otherwise, every one of our children is different from the majority in some way—whether it's religion, skin color, body type, financial situation, health, mental ability, etc. I constantly tell my children to honor that difference; indeed, from time to time, I casually point out what is different among all the families that we know. The real cruelty to a child is to fail to teach him how to deal with the unfairness and peer pressure that he will surely encounter no matter what his situation.

This is what I did prior to sending my preschooler off to school. One day, while playing with her, I put on a puppet show for her using little stick puppets. My story line revolved around a little girl who was vegan and got teased at school for bringing her own lunch and eating "different" food. The other children shunned her and wouldn't play with her. The little girl felt sad.

Then she noticed there were some other children who also were being left out, so she went over to them and made new friends. Eventually the teasing children saw the vegan child and her new friends having so much fun together that they realized they missed playing with her. Soon all the children were playing together and having lots of fun. Eventually the teasing children started asking serious questions about why the little girl was vegan, and admiring her for her choice. Partway through the puppet show, when the little girl was ostracized, my daughter's eyes started to get a little watery, but, at the end, her face lit up and with a big smile she said, "That little girl is just like me!" (I've since turned the puppet show into a children's picture book called *Sara's Ice Cream*.)

Often I play a game with my daughter called What Would You Do If… where we try to come up with different ways of dealing with the mean things children might say. Our game has paid off. One day my daughter came home from school and told me that some older boys had said that her food (we had sent yam sushi that day) smelled bad. "What did you do?" I asked her. "I just smiled and took another bite," she said.

I do realize that as adults my children may end up not being vegan or even vegetarian. That will be *their* choice. But I don't worry about depriving them of McDonald's burgers, or candy from trick or treating, or junk food at public events. I feel good about the fact that, while they are too young to fully appreciate the long-term consequences of their food choices, I am helping them to grow the healthiest bodies possible and establish strong neural connections in their brains that link happy times with healthful vegan foods rather than artificially colored and flavored, health-robbing rubbish.

During the preschool years, children identify heavily with their parents—so this is the time to teach, teach, teach! You shouldn't worry whether some concepts are too advanced for them, just look for "teachable moments" to instill in them your values and why these make sense to you. The essence of what you say will be absorbed, even if your child's intellect can't fully grasp all the details. Tell your children what the competing interests will argue and why you disagree; use your ever-changing environment to stimulate continuous discussion.

I know the day may come when my comments will be met with sarcastic replies or rolled eyes from my children. Then I will stop preaching. I'll know I've done my best to influence my children to adopt a healthy, compassionate lifestyle, and that it's time to back off a little and hope my efforts were sufficient. If my children become teens and start rebelling against our values and veganism, our home will remain a vegan sanctuary. I will know that I have done my best to give them a good foundation. I've made conscious choices for the well-being of my children and the biosphere they will inherit. I will know I have prepared them as best I could to deal with peer pressure and attacks from a culture that pushes us to be "consumers" instead of thinking individuals. Ultimately, however, it will be up to them.

Respecting Difference *and* Holding Tight

As I have said often throughout this book, there is no one right way to bring up a child. However, as any cultural anthropologist can confirm, some cultures, and by implication their cultural practices, seem to produce more happy, well-adjusted individuals than others.

In the oft-cited book *The Continuum Concept*, author Jean Liedloff writes about the traditional culture of a native people living deep in the rain forest of South America. Liedloff's descriptions of their lifestyle prior to significant exposure to Western culture embody many of the qualities that Americans seem to be longing for: values based upon a sense of family, community, cooperation, responsibility, *and* tolerance for the different ways others may choose to enjoy their freedom. Liedloff's study of this culture illuminated the kinds of experiences human beings require in infancy for optimal physical, mental, and emotional development. These are: constant physical contact with the mother or other caregiver, including sleeping in physical contact;[1] constantly being "in arms" while the person carrying the child goes on about his or her business; responding to the child's needs without undue attention; breastfeeding in response to the child's own body's signals; and sensing elders' expectations that the child is innately social, cooperative, and worthy, and has self-preservation instincts.

These types of experiences are most likely exactly what our species requires as a result of the adaptations we have experienced during our long period of evolution. Liedloff's work laid the foundation for the parenting style of William and Martha Sears's attachment-parenting.

Our children too can grow up to experience the birthright of evolved *Homo sapiens*. They can feel secure and loved as they see themselves a vital part of increasingly complex communities beginning with their family and extending to include all life. They can experience vibrant health as a result of long-term breastfeeding, a whole-foods, plant-based diet, and conscious choices about what else they are exposed to.

A compassionately raised child—one who has had a continuum- or attachment-style infancy, who has been taught to love a healthful, plant-based diet, and whose parents have made conscious choices regarding the wide array of technologies and cultural experiences available today—will have a good attention span with a creative imagination allowing her to learn and absorb the best of what humanity has to offer. She would be a good citizen, questioning everything and then making thoughtful decisions, exercising her freedom responsibly. He will be full of joy, interested in the world around him, and considerate of how his actions may affect others.

Western civilization took its first baby steps toward a more compassionate world when it embraced the ideas of Dr. Benjamin Spock. Today, I am filled with hope as our culture sits on the threshold of once again taking steps in the direction of compassion. While attachment-parenting is not yet as well-known as Dr. Spock's methods, the Searses' popularity is increasing. I predict we will soon have a critical mass of young people who were raised attachment-style.

As this new generation comes of age, the consequences of population growth and human destruction of the natural world will become so self-evident that the attempts by corporations and the military-industrial complex to put a positive spin on consumption will finally fade. The myth of a good life via unbridled materialism will be rejected by significant numbers, just as it was in the Sixties. Children who come from entirely authoritarian upbringings, with tenuous connections to their parents, will for the most part be compliant, following the path laid out by institutions. They will be followers.

The children raised attachment-style, however, with their energy, enthusiasm, and ability to think for themselves will be leaders in the next ideological revolution. The Sixties will come around in its next incarnation, only this time it will not be narrowly contained within the human sphere. We will extend our circle of compassion.

Cruelty and exploitation of nonhuman animals will take its rightful place as anathema to people of good conscience. The resulting changes will bring a new level of compassion and hope to humanity. This is my vision.[2]

Parenting is a joy and a responsibility. I believe that by working to raise our children as physically, emotionally, mentally, and spiritually healthy as possible we are giving them the best odds for a good life—whatever the future may bring. Humans are social creatures; we can only realize our full potential in the context of a supportive community. As parents, if we can successfully build a community that reinforces our values, and if we can by example show our children how to live a life that is compassionate and based upon conscious choices rather then just mindlessly following what we think everyone else is doing, then maybe our children, or perhaps our children's children, will be in a position to positively impact life on this planet for a long time to come. I have faith that the vast majority of children we raise this way or their descendants will be creators of a better world.

---

1. Sleeping in physical contact is the norm for most mammals, especially primates. It facilitates bonding, builds security, and makes breastfeeding easier.

2. In the final revision (he made before he died) of his classic book, *Dr. Spock's Baby and Child Care*, Benjamin Spock encouraged parents to nourish their children with a vegan diet. This was the very same diet he credited with improving his own health and prolonging his life.

Recipes

A WORD ABOUT INGREDIENTS FIRST. THERE ARE ONLY three pure fats that we use in food in our house. Because pesticide residues and other toxins tend to concentrate in fats, I am willing to spend a little extra and buy the organic versions of my oils, which I use sparingly anyway. For all cooking and all savory dishes I use organic extra virgin olive oil. For sweets (baked goods) where I don't want the olive oil flavor, I use organic canola oil. Flax oil, which does nothing for flavor, and is rapidly damaged by heat, light, and air but is an excellent source of the omega-3 fatty acids, I add to smoothies and use for salad dressings. I sometimes add flax oil at the last minute to dishes that aren't too hot.

In addition to animal products in your kitchen, the other big health robbers are trans-fats. You should read labels on all processed foods carefully to make sure there are no hydrogenated or partially hydrogenated fats and oils. In our family, we also avoid aspartame, artificial colors and flavors, and monosodium glutamate (MSG).

The following recipes are not intended as a substitute for a good all-around vegan cookbook. (See the Resources section for some suggestions.) The recipes I've included here are ones I've created and for which my family or friends repeatedly ask.

Asparagus in Lemon Mustard Sauce
Easy, elegant, low in fat, and tasty!

Ingredients

1 to 2 pounds fresh asparagus
3 tbs lemon juice
2 tbs maple syrup
1/2 cup water

1 tbs arrowroot powder
2 tbs Dijon mustard
1/4 tsp mustard powder
1/4 tsp salt

Instructions

Wash asparagus and break bottom two inches off each stalk. Place asparagus on vegetable steamer set in a covered pot with a half-inch of water in the bottom. Turn on high and bring to boil for about five minutes, until it just turns soft. Turn off heat and let sit, covered. Place all other ingredients in a cold pan and mix well with egg beater. Then heat over low heat, stirring frequently until it starts to bubble and thicken. Remove from heat. Arrange asparagus on a plate in a sunburst shape with spear heads out. Drizzle lemon-mustard sauce over asparagus and serve hot.

***

Berries and Tofu Cream
A simple and sweet finish for special dinners.

Ingredients

1 12.3 oz package, hard-style silken tofu
1/3 cup maple syrup
2 tsp natural vanilla
1/4 cup soy milk
2 cups frozen fruit, any combination of peaches, blueberries, cherries, raspberries, or strawberries

Instructions

Chop fruit into almond-size pieces while still frozen. Place first four ingredients into blender and blend until smooth. Chop fruit and put into a measuring cup until you have two full cups. Get four dessert cups and place a quarter of the fruit mixture into each cup while still frozen, then drizzle with a quarter of the tofu mixture. Place cups into refrigerator for at least one hour prior to serving. Garnish each cup with a cherry or strawberry on top.

***

Carotuna Wraps

During one of our raw food forays I was trying to find a good use for all of that leftover carrot pulp. This one is very popular too.

Ingredients

4 cups loosely packed carrot pulp (left over from a juicer)
5 tbs Bragg's Aminos (can substitute soy sauce)
2 tbs lemon juice
1 tbs onion powder
1 tsp kelp powder
1 cup finely chopped celery
3 soft, medium sized avocados (mashed)
1 head romaine or leaf lettuce broken into 2-by-3–inch pieces

Instructions

Place all ingredients except the lettuce into a large bowl and mix well. Then spoon about one to two tbs of this mixture (depending on size of lettuce leaf) onto a piece of lettuce and roll it up. Continue doing this until all the mixture is used up.

***

Carrots and Cabbage

A simple and colorful addition to any meal.

Ingredients

2 cups chopped red cabbage
2 cups thinly sliced carrots
1/2 cup water

2 tsp maple syrup
1/2 tsp Celtic sea salt

Instructions

Place ingredients in a covered pan. Heat on medium for five minutes.

***

Caesar Salad
Friends ask me for this recipe, more than any other.

<u>Ingredients (dressing)</u>

3 to 5 cloves of garlic
1/4 cup kalamata olives (pits removed)
1/4 cup water
3 tbs lemon juice

2 tbs soy sauce
3 tbs Dijon mustard
1/4 cup nutritional yeast

<u>Instructions</u>

Place the garlic, olives, water, lemon juice, and soy sauce into a blender. Put the lid on and blend on high until smooth. Add mustard and yeast and blend again. Stores well in fridge for at least a week.

<u>Ingredients (croutons)</u>

6 slices hearty whole-grain bread
1 tbs garlic powder
1 tsp salt
olive oil vegetable spray

2 tsp marjoram
1 tsp thyme
1 tsp ground rosemary

<u>Instructions</u>

Cut bread into small cubes and place in a very large bowl. Spray well with the vegetable oil spray and sprinkle with a third of the salt and herbs. Toss well. Repeat two more times until all the salt and herbs have been used. Transfer croutons to cookie sheet in a single layer, and place in oven at 200 degrees F for thirty minutes. Remove from oven and stir croutons and return to oven for another thirty minutes. Allow to cool. Then transfer to airtight container, if not using right away.

<u>Instructions (salad)</u>

Separate leaves from entire head of romaine lettuce; wash, and pat dry on clean towels. Tear leaves and place in bowl. Add croutons, cover with dressing, and toss. Serve immediately.

***

Chapati Roll-ups

Kids love bite-sized foods, even more so when they get to dip them as well!
Chapatis are Indian flatbread, although you can substitute burrito shells.

Ingredients

6 oz silken tofu hard-style (about 1/2 of a 12.3 oz package)
15 oz can garbanzo beans (drained)
1 tsp nutritional yeast
1 tbs Dijon mustard
1 tbs balsamic vinegar
1/2 tsp salt
6 grated carrots
1 package of six chapatis

Instructions

Place all ingredients except the carrots and the chapatis in the blender and
blend until smooth. Spread about two tbs of this mixture thinly over entire surface of chapati. Sprinkle a sixth of the grated carrots over the spread and roll
up. Cut into pieces like sushi and serve with remaining contents of blender for
dipping.

***

EFA Oatmeal

A great way to get omega-3 essential fatty acids into my children each day.
When preparing this for my younger child, I omit the maple syrup. The omega-
3 fatty acids found in flax oil are necessary for the brain, vision, and immune
system. DHA, which is now being touted for brain development, can be formed
in the body if there is adequate omega-3. Caution: Omega-3s are very perishable from heat, oxygen, and light. I always add the flax oil very last, right before
I serve it.

Ingredients

2 cups water
1/4 tsp Celtic sea salt
1 cup rolled oats
1 tsp vanilla

1/2 cup soy milk
1 to 2 tbs maple syrup to taste
2 tsp flaxseed oil

Instructions

Place salt in water and bring to boil. Add oatmeal and simmer on low, five to ten minutes until creamy. Remove from heat and add vanilla, soy milk, and maple syrup. Mix well. Right before serving add flax oil and mix well. (The essential fatty acids in the oil are very perishable, so make sure oatmeal is cooled slightly before adding, then eat it right away!)

***

Florentine Wraps

An elegant and tasty entrée. This dish is very simple if you use a bread machine to prepare the dough. You can either follow my bread machine recipe below, or any recipe of your choice that will yield one pound of whole wheat bread dough. My recipes use a soy cheese called Soymage. It is one of the few cheese alternatives that is 100 percent vegan. Read the labels and you will see that most contain casein, a dairy protein.

Ingredients (bread dough)
Place into bread machine pan the following in order.
1 1/3 cups of water
2 tbs olive oil
2 cups of whole wheat high-gluten (bread) flour
3/4 cup oat flour
1/4 cup gluten
1/4 cup Cajun Crystals (can substitute sugar)
1 tsp salt
2 tsp bread yeast

Instructions
Place machine on dough only cycle; when done (about ninety minutes later), remove and proceed.

Ingredients (filling)

1 tbs olive oil	1/4 cup packed fresh basil
2 medium onions (chopped)	1 tsp thyme
5 cloves garlic	1/2 tsp marjoram
4 10 oz boxes (frozen) spinach	1/2 tsp rosemary
3 tbs soy sauce	1 cup vegan mayonnaise
1/4 cup balsamic vinegar	8 to 9 oz of soy cheese (see above)

Instructions

Place olive oil in a large cast-iron skillet on high, add onions and sauté while stirring, until starting to brown. Add garlic and heat another two minutes. Add spinach (properly drained, or thawed if frozen), soy sauce, balsamic vinegar, and herbs. Turn heat down to medium and continue cooking and stirring occasionally until no liquid is left. Remove from heat and let sit uncovered for five minutes, then add the nayonnaise, mix well, and set aside.

Instructions (assembly)

Divide dough into four equal balls. Take one ball and roll into about a foot-long sausage shape, then use a rolling pin to roll out into a flat rectangle about 9 by 16 inches on an oiled surface. Spread a quarter of the spinach filling on the entire rectangle, except leave a 1-inch margin without filling. Then spread a quarter of the grated soy cheese over that. Roll up like a jelly roll (beginning at the long side), seal all open parts by pinching, including the seam, and set seam side down on an oiled cooking sheet. Repeat for each of the other remaining dough balls until you have four long "wraps." Place two per cookie sheet and set in a warm oven (about 150 degrees) and let rise for thirty to sixty minutes until double in size, then remove from oven, preheat oven to 350 and then bake for twenty-five minutes until lightly brown. Allow to cool ten minutes, then slice in 1-inch sections and serve.

***

Green Rice

When I was growing up, my mom used to make a wonderful casserole called green rice, which had broccoli, spinach, rice, egg, canned mushroom soup, and copious amounts of cheese. It was one of my "comfort foods." I was delighted when I found a way to recreate it as a vegan dish. I always make a lot, because everyone at my house eats a lot of it! Leftovers taste great cold too.

Ingredients

5 cups cooked brown rice (made from 2 1/2 cups dry)
2 heads broccoli steamed and then chopped
4 10 oz. frozen packages chopped spinach (thawed and drained)
1 large onion (chopped)
1 tsp + 1 tsp olive oil
1 12.3 oz box silken tofu
1 cup soy milk (unflavored variety)
1/3 cup soy sauce

2 tbs balsamic vinegar
1 tbs arrowroot powder (could substitute corn starch)
1 tsp garlic powder
1/4 tsp black pepper
1/4 tsp thyme
1/4 tsp mustard powder
pinch cayenne
8 oz Soymage cheddar style (grated)
3/4 cup raw wheat germ

Instructions
Preheat oven to 350 F. Heat 1 teaspoon of the oil in a skillet on medium high. Add the chopped onion and stir frequently until it starts to brown. Turn off heat and set aside. Place in the blender the following: silken tofu, soy milk, soy sauce, balsamic vinegar, arrowroot powder, garlic powder, black pepper, thyme, mustard powder, and cayenne. Blend until smooth. In a very large bowl combine the rice, broccoli, spinach, sautéed onions, and grated Soymage. Mix thoroughly. Pour contents of blender over all of this and mix until evenly distributed. Use the last teaspoon of olive oil to coat one very large or two medium baking dishes. Spoon contents of bowl into the oiled dish, top with the wheat germ, and spray lightly with vegetable spray. Bake in oven for thirty minutes.

***

Herbed Raspberry Dressing
A quick, delicious topping for your tossed salads, full of essential fatty acids!

Ingredients
12 oz can frozen raspberry juice
3 cloves raw garlic (chopped)
1 tbs prepared yellow mustard
1/4 cup rice vinegar
2 tbs balsamic vinegar

3 tbs flax oil
1/4 cup packed fresh basil (chopped)
1/2 tsp fresh rosemary leaves
1 tbs fresh parsley (chopped)
1/2 of a small onion (chopped)

Instructions
Place all ingredients in a blender and blend well. Use on any salad, especially good over a bed of fresh arugula!

***

Israeli Salad

When my family visited Israel when I was child, something like this salad was served there with breakfast, lunch, and dinner.

<u>Ingredients</u>
4 medium cucumbers (peeled if not organic)
1 lb tomatoes
1 large green pepper
10 oz jar chopped pimento-stuffed green olives
10 to 12 scallions
6 tbs lemon juice
1 tsp garlic powder
1/4 tsp thyme
1 tsp onion powder

<u>Instructions</u>
Cut cucumber, tomatoes, and green pepper into almond-sized pieces and place in a large bowl. Remove root tips from scallions and dice and add to bowl. Add entire jar of olives including liquid. Add remaining ingredients and mix well.

***

Jojo's Baked Potatoes

Remember baked potatoes with sour cream? Here's a vegan version that's been a huge hit with everyone we've tried it on!

<u>Ingredients</u>
6 to 8 russet potatoes (preferably organic, well-scrubbed)
1 12.3 oz package of hard-style aseptic tofu
1 tbs lemon juice
2 tbs rice vinegar
1/2 tsp salt
pepper
1 tbs soy sauce

<u>Instructions</u>
Place potatoes in oven and heat on 400 degrees F until soft (about forty-five to ninety minutes, depending upon their size). Remove from oven, slice length-

wise, and open up on a plate. Make ten to twelve more cuts widthwise across potato, top with two to three tbs of tofu topping, sprinkle with pepper and soy sauce, and serve while still hot.

***

Lox Bagel and Cream Cheese

When I was growing up, this was a favorite in my family. After I became vegan, it was one of the few meals I really missed. This alternative is truly satisfying. Mirin is a sweet Japanese saki found in macrobiotic section of natural foods groceries.

Ingredients
Whole wheat bagels
10 oz jar roasted red peppers, sliced into 1-inch-thick strips
Bagel spread:

1 lb firm water-packed tofu	2 tbs white zinfandel
7 tbs mellow white miso	1 tbs garlic powder
5 tbs Mirin	2 tsp marjoram
3 tbs lemon juice	1/2 tsp thyme

Instructions
Remove the tofu and set it in a thick towel and squeeze until it crumbles, removing as much of the liquid as possible. Then place in a food processor or blender. Add all the remaining ingredients in the bagel spread and mix until a homogeneous creamy mixture. (If using a blender, this will require repeatedly stopping it and mixing with a long spoon and then blending again.) Slice bagels in half and toast them. Remove from toaster, slather with bagel spread, and arrange a thin layer of red pepper on top. Serve on a bed of lettuce with slices of tomato and onion on the side.

***

Marinated Cucumber slices

I can *never* keep these on hand. As soon as the kids find out about them, they are *gone!*

Ingredients

2 large cucumbers	2 cups water
1 small onion (sliced)	1/4 cup cane-juice crystals or sugar
3 cloves garlic (chopped)	2 tsp salt
1 cup apple-cider vinegar	2 tsp dill weed

Instructions

Wash cucumbers. If they are *not* organic, peel them; otherwise leave the skin on. Slice and place them into a large covered dish. Add and mix all remaining ingredients. Allow them to sit covered in the refrigerator for 24 hours (if you can!) before serving. When the cucumber slices are all eaten, the marinade can be reused by adding a little fresh garlic, onion and vinegar.

***

Minted Carrots

Not the way we usually eat carrots, just a special occasional treat.

Ingredients

6 medium carrots (scrubbed and sliced thin)
1/2 cup water
2 tbs maple syrup
2 tsp mint leaves (chopped)
1 tsp arrowroot powder or corn starch
1 tsp water

Instructions

Place carrots, 1/2 cup water, maple syrup, and mint in a covered pot and heat on medium for five minutes. Turn off heat and let sit for two minutes. Mix the arrowroot powder with 1 tsp water until dissolved. Pour off liquid from the carrots, and add the arrowroot mixture to it; mix well and return to pot with carrots. Heat carrots on medium for about a minute, stirring continuously until liquid thickens. Serve warm.

***

Pregnant Momma Protein Shake

I drank one of these every day during my last trimester. If you can find alternative types of protein powder (i.e., soy, rice, oat, etc.), it would be good to rotate these and on those days that your protein powder is not soy based, omit the tofu and trade in the soy milk for juice, rice milk, or nut milk. This decreases the possibility of your baby becoming sensitized to soy.

Ingredients

1 cup soy milk (B-12 enriched)
1/2 package silken tofu
1 tbs frozen juice concentrate (strawberry-guava, or raspberry, or peach-mango work best)

1 frozen banana (peel and slice before freezing)
1/2 cup other frozen fruit (peaches or berries work well)
1 tbs flaxseed oil
1 tsp vanilla
1 scoop vegan protein powder
1 tsp spirulina or blue-green algae

Instructions
Place all ingredients in the blender and blend until smooth; drink immediately. (Caution: you may wish to decrease or omit the flaxseed oil the last three weeks prior to your due date, since omega-3 fatty acids are the precursors for a type of prostaglandin that may inhibit the start of labor. Studies show that women consuming lots of fish high in omega-3s had a high risk of "post-due" pregnancies.)

***

Quick-Browned Tofu
Makes a quick snack all by itself; or place it between two pieces of bread, with mustard and lettuce.

Ingredients

1/2 pound water-packed hard tofu	1 tbs water
vegetable spray	2 tsp soy sauce
1 tsp olive oil	1 tsp nutritional yeast (optional)

Instructions
Slice tofu into 1/4-inch-thick slices. Lay slices on a clean dry towel, fold towel over tofu and gently press down, and hold for a moment to absorb excess moisture. Using a nonstick skillet, spray pan lightly with vegetable spray, add olive oil, and heat over medium flame. Add pressed tofu. Allow to brown slightly, then turn over and brown other side. Mix water, soy sauce, and nutritional yeast in a small cup and dump all at once into skillet, while turning tofu back and forth until all moisture is absorbed. Remove from heat and serve.

***

Simple Lentils
A quick and easy dish. Serve with brown rice, a steamed vegetable, and a salad for a complete meal.

Ingredients
2 cups green or brown lentils (picked over and rinsed)
5 cups water
1 large onion (diced)
3 bay leaves
2 tsp Bragg's Aminos

Instructions
Place all ingredients except amino acids in a covered pot and bring to boil. Simmer thirty minutes, stirring occasionally. Remove bay leaves and add amino acids and serve.

***

Tofu and Cabbage
This one is quick and easy, and a favorite of my children. I use a cast-iron skillet with glass lid to prepare this dish.

Ingredients

1 onion (chopped)	1/4 cup lemon juice
1 head purple cabbage (chopped)	1 tsp dried rosemary
1 tbs olive oil	2 tsp marjoram
1 lb firm water-packed tofu	1 tsp thyme
1/4 cup soy sauce	sprinkle of cayenne

Instructions
Slice tofu into pieces about a third of an inch thick and press gently between clean dry towels, then dice tofu into little cubes and set in a bowl. Add all remaining ingredients except the cabbage, onion, and oil. Stir well, allow to marinate, and set aside. (This step can be done hours or even a day ahead and will greatly improve the flavor.)

Chop onion and sauté in the oil until it starts to brown. Remove tofu, using a slotted spoon (or else pour through a strainer and save the marinade). Turn heat to high and then add the tofu. Mix frequently until it starts to brown. Then add the remaining marinade juices, and put on the lid. Allow to cook for about three to four minutes while you chop the cabbage.

Add the cabbage, mix well, put the lid back on, and turn the heat down. Stir every few minutes until cabbage softens slightly. Serve over brown rice or pasta.

***

Vegetable Stew

A great comfort dish! Hearty, low in fat, and full of vegetables!

Ingredients

1 tbs olive oil
3 onions (coarsely chopped)
15 cloves garlic (peeled and chopped)
5 bay leaves
2 cups chopped celery
1 1/2 cups green lentils
1 cup red lentils
3 medium potatoes cut into small chunks

12 cups water
5 cups thinly chopped carrots
1 cup chopped cauliflower
2 cups chopped red cabbage
3 tbs Bragg's Aminos
2 tbs Mirin
1/4 cup light yellow miso
1 cup frozen corn kernels
1 cup frozen green beans

Instructions

In a large pot, heat olive oil and then add onions, and stir until starting to brown. Add garlic and stir another two minutes. Add water, bay leaves, green lentils, red lentils, and potatoes. Bring to boil and cook covered for thirty-five minutes. Find and remove the five bay leaves. Add the carrots, cauliflower, cabbage, Bragg's Aminos, and Mirin and simmer for five minutes. Place the miso in a small bowl and add broth from the stew to it one tablespoon at a time, mixing until it makes about a cup of liquid; then add this liquid to the stew and mix well. Add the corn and green beans, stir well for two minutes, and turn off the heat. Serve hot.

Bibliography

The following books were either referenced in *Compassionate Souls* or else are sources of additional information on topics I have touched upon. While I have found something of value in each of these books, their inclusion is not necessarily an endorsement of them in their entirety.

Books on Pregnancy, Birth, Breastfeeding, and Parenting

Arms, Suzanne. *Immaculate Deception: A New Look at Women and Childbirth in America* (Boston: Houghton Mifflin, 1975).

Baldwin, Rahima. *Special Delivery: The Complete Guide to Informed Birth* (Berkeley, CA: Celestial Arts, 1979).

Baumslag, Naomi, and Dia L. Michels. *Milk, Money, and Madness: The Culture and Politics of Breastfeeding* (Westport, CT: Bergin and Garvey, 1995).

Cohen, Nancy Wainer, and Lois J. Estner. *Silent Knife: Cesarean Prevention and Vaginal Birth after Cesarean.* (S. Hadley, MA: Bergin and Garvey, 1983).

Coloroso, Barbara. *Kids Are Worth It!: Giving Your Child the Gift of Inner Discipline* (New York: Avon, 1994).

Dreikurs, Rudolph. *Children: The Challenge* (New York: Hawthorn/Dutton, 1964).

Faber, Adele, and Elaine Mazlish. *Siblings without Rivalry: How to Help Your Children Live Together So You Can Live Too* (New York: Avon, 1987).

Gaskin, Ina May. *Spiritual Midwifery* (Summertown, TN: The Book Publishing Co., 1977).

Huggins, Kathleen, and Linda Ziedrich. *The Nursing Mother's Guide to Weaning* (Boston: Harvard Common, 1994).

Jones, Sandy. *Crying Baby, Sleepless Nights* (New York: Warner, 1983).

Kitzinger, Sheila. *Breastfeeding Your Baby* (New York: Knopf, 1989).

——. *The Complete Book of Pregnancy and Childbirth* (New York: Knopf, 1980).

——. *Home Birth* (New York: Dorling-Kindersley, 1991).

——. *Ourselves as Mothers: The Universal Experience of Motherhood* (London: Bantam, 1993).

Korte, Diana. *A Good Birth, a Safe Birth* (Harvard: Harvard Common, 1992).

La Leche League International. *The Womanly Art of Breastfeeding* (New York: Plume, 1997).

Liedloff, Jean. *The Continuum Concept* (New York: Knopf, 1977).

Rosemond, John K. *John Rosemond's Six-Point Plan for Raising Happy, Healthy Children* (Kansas City, MO: Andrews and McMeel, 1990).

Sears, William, M.D. *Nighttime Parenting: How to Get Your Baby and Child to Sleep* (New York: Plume, 1999).

Sears, William, M.D., and Martha Sears. *The Baby Book: Everything You Need to Know about Your Baby from Birth to Age Two* (Boston: Little Brown, 1993).

——. *The Birth Book: Everything You Need to Know to Have a Safe and Satisfying Birth* (Boston: Little Brown ,1994).

——. *The Discipline Book: Everything You Need to Know to Have a Better-Behaved Child* (Boston: Little Brown, 1995).

——. *Parenting the Fussy Baby and High-Need Child: Everything You Need to Know from Birth to Age Five* (Boston: Little Brown, 1996).

Solter, Aletha J. *The Aware Baby: A New Approach to Parenting* (Goleta, CA: Shining Star, 1998).

Spock, Benjamin, and Steven J. Parker. *Dr. Spock's Baby and Child Care* (New York: Pocket, 1998).

Thevenin, Tine. *The Family Bed: An Age-Old Concept in Child Rearing* (Minneapolis: Thevenin, 1977).

Books on Vegetarianism and Veganism

Akers, Keith, *A Vegetarian Sourcebook* (Denver, CO: Vegetarian Press, 1993).

Havala, Suzanne, *The Complete Idiot's Guide to Being Vegetarian* (New York: Alpha Books, 1999).

Klaper, Michael, M.D. *Pregnancy, Children and the Vegan Diet* (Umatilla, FL: Gentle World, 1987).

——. *Vegan Nutrition: Pure and Simple* (Umatilla, FL: Gentle World, 1987).

Robbins, John. *Diet for a New America* (Walpole, NH: Stillpoint, 1987).

Rowe, Martin, ed. *The Way of Compassion: Survival Strategies for a World in Crisis* (New York: Stealth Technologies, 1999).

Stepaniak, Joanne, M.S.Ed. *The Vegan Sourcebook* (Lincolnwood, IL: Lowell House, 1998).

Wasserman, Debra, and Reed Mangels. *Vegan Handbook: Over 200 Delicious Recipes, Meal Plans and Vegetarian Resources for All Ages* (Baltimore, MD: Vegetarian Resource Group, 1996).

Books on Animal Rights

Davis, Karen. *Prisoned Chickens, Poisoned Eggs: An Inside Look at the Modern Poultry Industry* (Summertown, TN: Book Publishing Co., 1996).

Eisnitz, Gail. *Slaughterhouse: The Shocking Story of Greed, Neglect and Inhumane Treatment Inside the U.S. Meat Industry* (Amherst, NY: Prometheus Books, 1997).

Mason, Jim, and Peter Singer. *Animal Factories* (New York: Harmony, 1990).

Regan, Tom. *The Case for Animal Rights* (Philadelphia: Temple University Press, 1983).

Singer, Peter. *Animal Liberation* (New York: Avon, 1990).

Books on the Environment and Health

Attwood, Charles R., M.D. *Dr. Attwood's Low-Fat Prescription for Kids* (New York: Viking Penguin, 1995).

Barnard, Neal, M.D. *How the New Four Food Groups Can Save Your Life* (New York: Harmony, 1993).

———. *The Power of Your Plate* (Summertown, TN: Book Publishing Co., 1990).

Cohen, Robert. *Milk the Deadly Poison* (Englewood Cliffs, NJ: Argus Publishing, 1998).

Colborn, Theo, Dianne Dumanowski, and John Peterson Myers. *Our Stolen Future: Are We Threatening Our Fertility, Intelligence and Survival?* (New York: Dutton, 1996).

.Coulter, Harris L. and Barbara Loe Fisher. *A Shot in the Dark: Why the P in the DPT Vaccination May Be Hazardous to Your Child's Health* (Garden City Park, NY: Avery, 1987).

Hulse, Virgil, M.D. *Mad Cows and Milk Gate* (Phoenix, OR: Marble Mountain Publishing, 1996).

Levitt, Blake B. *Electromagnetic Fields: A Consumer's Guide to the Issues and How to Protect Ourselves* (New York: Harcourt Brace, 1995).

Lyman, Howard. *Mad Cowboy: Plain Truth from the Cattle Rancher Who Won't Eat Meat* (New York: Scribner, 1998).

McDougall, John A., M.D. *The McDougall Program: Twelve Days to Dynamic Health* (New York: New American Library, 1990).

———. *The McDougall Program for Women: What Every Woman Needs to Know to Be Healthy for Life* (New York: Dutton, 1999).

Mendelsohn, Robert S., M.D. *How to Raise a Healthy Child in Spite of Your Doctor* (New York: Ballantine, 1987).

———. *Male Practice: How Doctors Manipulate Women* (Chicago: Contemporary Books Inc, 1982).

Miller, Neil Z. *Vaccines: Are They Really Safe and Effective?* (Sante Fe, NM: New Atlantean Press, 1992).

Neustaedter, Randall. *The Immunization Decision: A Guide for Parents* (Berkeley, CA: North Atlantic, 1990).

Northrup, Christiane. *Women's Bodies, Women's Wisdom: Creating Physical and Emotional Health and Healing* (New York: Bantam, 1998).

Ott, John N. *Health and Light* (New York: Pocket, 1976).

Radetsky, Peter. *Allergic to the Twentieth Century: The Explosion in Environmental Allergies* (Boston: Little Brown, 1997).

Scheibner, Viera, Ph.D. *Vaccination: 100 Years of Orthodox Research Shows That Vaccines Represent a Medical Assault on the Immune System* (Maryborough, Australia: Australian Print Group, 1993).

Schmidt, Michael A. *Smart Fats: How Dietary Fats and Oils Affect Mental, Physical and Emotional Intelligence* (Berkeley, CA: Frog Ltd, 1997).

Whitaker, Julian M., M.D. *Reversing Heart Disease* (New York: Warner, 1985).

Books on Politics, Culture, and Families

Crossen, Cynthia. *Tainted Truth: The Manipulation of Fact in America* (New York: Simon and Schuster, 1994).

Gilbert, Roberta M. *Extraordinary Relationships: A New Way of Thinking about Human Interactions.* (Minneapolis: Chronimed Publishing, 1992).

Havala, Suzanne, M.S., R.D. *Good Foods, Bad Foods: What's Left to Eat?* (Minneapolis: Chronimed Publishing, 1998).

Hightower, Jim. *There's Nothing in the Middle of the Road but Yellow Stripes and Dead Armadillos* (New York: HarperCollins, 1997).

Kerr, Michael E. *Family Evaluation: An Approach Based on Bowen Theory* (New York: Norton, 1988).

Korten, David C. *When Corporations Rule the World* (San Francisco: Berrett-Koehler Publishers, Inc., 1995).

Lerner, Harriet Goldhor. *The Dance of Anger: A Woman's Guide to Changing the Patterns of Intimate Relationships* (New York: HarperPerennial, 1985).

———. *The Mother Dance: How Children Change Your Life* (New York: HarperCollins, 1988).

Mander, Jerry. *Four Arguments for the Elimination of Television* (New York: Quill, 1978).

Mason, Jim. *An Unnatural Order: Why We Are Destroying the Planet and Each Other* (New York: Continuum, 1998).

Moran, Victoria. *Shelter for the Spirit: How to Make Your Home a Haven in a Hectic World* (New York: HarperCollins, 1997).

Nearing, Helen. *The Good Life: Helen and Scott Nearing's Sixty Years of Self-Sufficient Living* (New York: Schocken, 1989).

Pipher, Mary Bray. *The Shelter of Each Other: Rebuilding Our Families* (New York: Ballantine, 1997).

Winn, Marie. *The Plug-in Drug* (New York: Viking Press, 1977).

Books on Education

Colfax, David. *Homeschooling for Excellence* (New York: Warner, 1988).

Dobson, Linda. *The Homeschooling Book of Answers: The 88 Most Important Questions Answered by Homeschooling's Most Respected Voices.* (Rocklin, CA: Prima Publishing, 1998).

Griffith, Mary. *The Unschooling Handbook: How to Use the Whole World as Your Child's Classroom* (Rocklin, CA: Prima Publishing, 1998).

Holt, John. *How Children Learn* (New York: Dell, 1967).

Pearce, Joseph Chilton. *Magical Child* (New York: Bantam, 1980).

Spietz, Heidi Anne. *Montessori at Home: A Complete Guide to Teaching Your Preschooler at Home Using the Montessori Method* (Rossmoor, CA: American Montessori Consulting, 1991).

Recommended Recipe Books

Bergeron, Ken. *Professional Vegetarian Cooking* (New York: John Wiley, 1999).

Hagler, Louise, and Dorothy R. Bates. *The New Farm Vegetarian Cookbook* (Summertown, TN: Book Publishing Co., 1975).

McDougall, Mary. *The McDougall Health-Supporting Cookbook: Volume One* (Clinton, NJ: New Win, 1985).

Nishimoto, Miyoko. *The Now and Zen Epicure: Gourmet Cuisine for the Enlightened Palate* (Summertown, TN: Book Publishing Co., 1991).

Raymond, Jennifer. *Fat-Free and Easy* (Calistoga, CA: Heart and Soul, 1995).

Saks, Anne, and Faith Stone. *The Shoshoni Cookbook: Vegetarian Recipes from the Shoshoni Yoga Retreat* (Summertown, TN: Book Publishing Co., 1993).

Sass, Lorna J. *Recipes from an Ecological Kitchen: Healthy Meals for You and the Planet* (New York: William Morrow, 1992).

Stepaniak, Joanne. *The Uncheese Cookbook: Creating Amazing Dairy-Free Cheese Substitutes and Classic "Uncheese" Dishes* (Summertown, TN: Book Publishing Co., 1994).

Stepaniak, Joanne, and Kathy Hecker. *Ecological Cooking: Recipes to Save the Planet* (Summertown, TN: Book Publishing Co., 1991).

Wagner, Lindsay, and Ariane Spade. *The High Road to Health: A Vegetarian Cookbook* (New York: Prentice Hall, 1990).

Suggested Books with a Compassionate Theme for Young Children

The Lorax, by Dr. Seuss (New York: Random House, 1971).
A classic. This is the story of Mr. Onceler, who comes upon a beautiful place where charming animals abound in the water, trees, and sky, and the land is filled with the incredible truffula trees. It turns out that the trees are quite useful for making thneeds (which everyone needs) and, in no time at all, Mr. Onceler has built a huge factory and is rapidly chopping the trees down. Everyone loves what Mr. Onceler has done, except for one character—the Lorax—who claims to speak for the trees (as well as the animals). He tells the Onceler, "Sir you are crazy with greed." Told in Dr. Seuss's fantastic rhyming fashion, the book will appeal to adults as much as children.

The Goose That Almost Got Cooked, by Marc Simont (New York: Scholastic, 1997).
Beautifully illustrated, with a simple text, Simont's book tells of a wild goose who loses her flock and stumbles upon a farm. The goose is amazed at the easy life these "captive" geese have—they are well-fed and get put safely in the barn each night. She decides to stay, until one day she learns the ugly truth—just in time!

A Home for Henny, by Karen Davis (Machipongo, VA: United Poultry Concerns, 1998).
A story that helps children (and parents) understand the problems with school hatching projects and follows the life of one particular chick who is luckier than most.

Madeline and The Bad Hat, by Ludwig Bemelmans (New York: Viking, 1957).
This story is about a mean little boy who moves in next door to Madeline's boarding school. As the child of an ambassador, he is a master at charming the adults, but Madeline sees through him, and is disgusted with his abuse of ani-

mals. One of the boy's nasty tricks backfires and ends up hurting *him*. Madeline and her teacher rescue him, but, while all the adults fawn over the boy and his injuries, Madeline tells him he deserved it. In the end he changes—"Lo and behold, the little barbarian turned into a vegetarian."

Leprechaun Cake and Other Tales—A Vegetarian Story Cookbook, by Vonnie Winslow Crist (Baltimore: Vegetarian Resource Group, 1995). A fun introduction to vegetarian cooking for children that weaves in fantasy with healthful vegetarian recipes.

Zeralda's Ogre, by Tommy Ungerer (Boulder, CO: Roberts Rinhart, 1999).
One of my friends thought this book unsuitable for her young children, but I *loved* it. It's a fairy tale about an ogre who loves to eat children, but is so charmed and well-fed by one sweet (but naive) little girl, Zeralda, that he comes to give up people-eating. The parallels to humans eating animals are unmistakable. Nicely illustrated.

The Girl Who Loved Caterpillars, by Jean Merrill (Topeka, KS: Econo-clad Books, 1999).
The story of a Japanese girl who treats caterpillars with respect and eschews all customs she doesn't consider "natural." Although her parents and servants are embarrassed by her ways, others are attracted to her and respect her. She's a great role model—setting an example of being true to yourself even if it runs contrary to the larger culture. Great pictures, lengthy text.

Forest Child, by Marni McGee (New York: Simon & Schuster, 1999).
About a young boy who is lost in the woods. At first the animals shun him because he is human. But when the animals see him free a rabbit caught in a trap, they all pitch in to care for the little boy until he can be returned to his human family. Gorgeous illustrations.

The Story of a Dolphin, by Katherine Orr (Minneapolis: Carolrhoda Books, 1995).
Based upon the true story of a wild dolphin who befriends some people. Misunderstandings between the dolphin and the growing numbers of humans who come to swim with her almost lead to her being killed, but fortunately a dolphin expert is able to help the humans learn how to treat her with respect, and the problems disappear.

Victor the Vegetarian, by Radha Vignola (Santa Cruz: AVIVA, 1994).
The story of Victor, who learns that the little lambs he loves are destined to be his dinner. It then occurs to him that he would probably love all the animals he eats if he got to know them too.

Miss Spider's Tea Party, by David Kirk (New York: Scholastic, 1994).
Whimsical story of Miss Spider, who is lonely because none of the insects will come to her tea party (fearing she will eat them). As it turns out, Miss Spider really *loves* insects and will only eat plants! All ends happily.

178

Resources

Online Resources

Sites with Information on Diet

www.living-foods.com/articles/. Articles on living foods.

www.meat.org. Excellent, though not for the fainthearted.

www.milkgate.com. Site based upon the book by Dr. Virgil Hulse, *Mad Cows and Milk Gate*.

www.navs-online.org. North American Vegetarian Society.

www.rawfood.com. Information on books available to get started learning about the optimum way of eating.

www.vegfamily.com. A site for vegetarian and vegan families, full of ideas and lots of parent-to-parent support.

www.veg.org. The vegetarian pages.

www.vegsource.com. One address with links to an exhaustive number of home pages from some of the most well-known speakers and writers on topics including health, nutrition, animal rights, and the environment.

www.vivavegie.org. Organization that publishes "101 Reasons Why I'm a Vegetarian". A great read.

www.vrg.org. The Vegetarian Resource Group

Sites About Parenting

www.alternamoms.com. Good assortment of info on pregnancy, birth, ultrasound, circumcision, vaccinations, and more.

www.awareparenting.com/english.htm. The home page for the work and writings of Aletha Solter, author of *The Aware Baby*.

www.bestfed.com. Breastfeeding, attachment-parenting, and more—with links to many other related subjects.

www.bradleybirth.com. Official Web site for Bradley childbirth education.

www.compleatmother.com. Magazine similar to the printed periodical *The Compleat Mother*. Supports natural childbirth, homebirth, pregnancy, attachment-parenting, not circumcising, not vaccinating, and more. Loaded with stories, humor, and anecdotes.

www.continuum-concept.org. Home page for the site based upon the book *The Continuum Concept*. These ideas form the basis for much of attachment-parenting. Must reading for every would-be parent!

www.lalecheleague.org. La Leche League. An excellent site with lots of wonderful information and support, plus links to other sites.

www.mothering.com. Online site for *Mothering Magazine*.

www.nurturing.ca/home.htm. Online version of *Nurturing Magazine*. Extremely comprehensive. Wonderful articles covering a range of alternative parenting ideas, plus lots of terrific links!

www.thenurturingparent.com. International site of the Natural Child Project, dedicated to a world where all children are treated with dignity, respect, understanding, and compassion.

Vaccination

www.avn.org.au. The Australian Vaccination Network. Great site with comprehensive information, medical journal articles, and stories and pictures of vaccine-injured people. Many links—including topics far beyond vaccination!

www.nextcity.com/contents/summer99/16shots.html. An especially good article entitled "Shots in the Dark," one of the best overviews of the history of vaccination and the major objections being raised against compulsory vaccination I've seen.

www.909shot.com. The National Vaccine Injury Center. Up-to-date information on all currently used routine childhood vaccinations.

www.thinktwice.com/global.htm. Comprehensive information about vaccines. Also lists numerous references in medical journals.

www.vaccines.net. The Vaccine Safety Website. Another great site with peer-reviewed journal references.

www.whale.to/vaccines/Mendelsohn.html. Article on vaccines from Robert Mendelsohn M.D. "The Medical Time Bomb of Immunization against Disease."

Television

www.sover.net/~gmws/untv/index.htm. The Un-TV guide sponsored by the Green Mountain Waldorf School. Includes some good articles about the dangers of television viewing as well as help to turn off the television.

www.tvfa.org. TV free America site. Has some excellent articles. Also has some links to other excellent sites.

www.whitedot.org. An interesting site, either based in or with ties to the UK, dedicated to getting people to turn off their televisions.

Environment and Sustainability

www.envirolink.com. A grassroots, online community linking hundreds of organizations in over 150 countries, with the most up-to-date environmental resources available. Includes links to animal rights too.

http://greenliving.org/inyourhome/. Useful information to help you protect your family from risks associated with chemicals—including those found in disposable diapers.

www.igc.org/mothers/. Home page for Mothers and Others, a group working to promote consumer choices that are safe and ecologically sustainable. Exceptional listing of links to a variety of subjects that go far beyond the discussion in *Compassionate Souls*, but will be of interest to readers.

www.newdream.org. Home page for the Center for a New American Dream, an organization working for sustainability. Articles address a wide range of issues including community, the environment, justice, government, agriculture, business, commercialism, and much more.

www.osf-facts.org. Based upon the book *Our Stolen Future*. For those who love science, enjoy detail, and want comprehensive data to balance antienvironmentalist rhetoric.

Education

www.angelfire.com/mo/sassafrassgrove. Sassafrass Grove Homeschooling site. Very comprehensive, with tons of links. Covers basic questions like the why and how of homeschooling as well as extensive support and resources for those who are already successfully homeschooling.

www.gomilpitas.com/homeschooling/methods/Waldorf.htm. The A to Z Home's Cool Page, all about Waldorf education. Lots of links, with a variety of points of view.

www.learninfreedom.org. General homeschooling site that proclaims, "School Is Dead, Learn in Freedom!" Lots of great information and links.

www.montessori.edu. The international Montessori Index. The official international Web site with information on the materials, methods, finding schools, and links to related sites.

http://unschooling.com. A site that will answer questions about what "unschooling" is and how to do it.

The Family Empowerment Institute, 2545 Koshkonong Road, Stoughton, WI 53589-2720. Tel.: 608-837-7577

Companies That Sell Wooden Toys

First Toys: 800-210-7318, www.firsttoys.com
Hand in Hand: 800-872-9745
North Star Toys: 800-737-0112
Rosie Hippo's: Wooden Toys 800-385-2620
Season's Natural Toys: 215-489-8697
TC Timber: 800-468-6873, www.tctimber.com

Periodicals

Ahimsa. American Vegan Society, PO Box 369, 56 Dinshah Lane, Malaga, NJ 08328. 856-694-2887

The Complete Mother. Jody McLaughlin ed., pub, PO Box 209, Minot, ND 58702-0209. 701-852-2822. www.compleatmother.com

Mothering Magazine. PO Box 1690, Sante Fe, NM 87504. 505-984-8116

Food and Water Journal. 389 Vermont Route 215, Walden, VT 05873. 802-563-3300

The Green Guide: Mothers and Others for a Livable Planet. 40 West 20th St., New York, NY 10011-4211. 888-ECO-INFO ext 301

Good Medicine. Physicians Committee for Responsible Medicine, 5100 Wisconsin Ave. NW, Suite 404, Washington, DC 20016. 202-686-2210. www.pcrm.org

Satya. PO Box 138, New York, NY 10012. 212-674-0952. www.stealthtechnologies.com/satya

Vegetarian Voice. North American Vegetarian Society, PO Box 72, Dolgeville, NY 13329. 518-568-7970

Vegetarian Journal. The Vegetarian Resource Group, PO Box 146, Baltimore, MD 21203. 410-366-8343

Vegetarian Times. 4 High Ridge Park, Dtamford, CT 06905 www.vegetariantimes.com

Yes! A Journal of Positive Futures. PO Box 10818, Bainbridge Island, WA 98110. 206-842-0216. www.futurenet.org